The Chicagoization of America

1893-1917

The Chicagoization of America

1893-1917

by Kenan Heise

GOLDEN DOOR OF TRANSPORTATION BUILDING

In a special way, the golden door of the Transportation Building at the World's Columbian Exposition became the magic door through which the Chicago idea of a democratic culture burst into the world. It was the antithesis of the borrowed culture that surrounded it at the 1893 world's fair and a fresh, strong representation of what America has to offer.

Other books by Kenan Heise:

They Speak for themselves: Interviews with the Destitute of Chicago

The Death of Christmas
(with Arthur Allan)

Is There Only One Chicago

How to Survive in Chicago and Enjoy It
(with Charles McWhinnie, Judith Birnbaum and Juanita Carlson)

The Journey of Silas B. Bigelow;

Chicago: Center for Enterprise
(with Michael Edgerton)

Aunt Ella Stories

Hands on Chicago
(with Mark Frazel)

and

Alphonse: A Play About Al Capone in His Own Words.

10 9 8 7 6 5 4 3 2 1

ISBN: 0-924772-01-8

Chicago Historical Bookworks
831 Main St.
Evanston, IL 60202

Printed in the United States

Layout and design by Dan Heise

Cover by Dorothy Kavka

To Chicago itself,
an idea and a metropolis

ACKNOWLEDGEMENTS

Special thanks to all those who helped turn this effort into a book. They include: Scott Holingue; Sterno; Ruth Ritchie; Carol, Tiger, and Ben Heise; John Lux; Ruth Buck; Ted Zelewsky and the staff of Print III and Mike Hirsch and the people at Whitehall Company.

Preface

Gene Fowler once described journalism as "history shot on the wing." As far as this definition is true — Kenan Heise is the journalist among us with the steadiest hand and the surest shooting piece. The only problem with extending this metaphor is that history is never killed in Kenan's hands. He catches it and then lets it go, like those fishermen who love fishing but cannot abide killing.

Kenan writes history and journalism and fiction and brings to each perspective a dogged gentleness that is never softminded, even when it is deservingly sentimental.

When he is is not writing books like this one, he divides his time between selling books in his unique book shop in Evanston where the Midwest—and Chicago in particular—provide all the grist he needs and in writing for the Chicago Tribune.

He specializes in obituaries, not as the dull, dreaded work assigned to someone on the nightshift because some momentary bigshot shuffled off his coil between editions but as lovingly erected milestones marking the end of long and interesting journeys. There are some of us who read a Kenan Heise obit just because his name is bylined, even if we are unacquainted with the honoree. Invariably, we are glad we stopped to read the marker. His elegies, full of country churchyard simplicity, are more remarkable for being etched in a word processor in the hubbub of a big city newsroom.

His fictions come from twice-told tales of simple people who order simple lives despite the easier chaos all around them. There is humor here (and in his non-fiction) a wryness more effective for its kind insistence. Kenan has a large shaggy head and peers through glasses which make his eyes seem larger than they are. All the better to see larger worlds, even in small events.

All his details can fit into small words, the better to carry his larger freight. You never really hear Kenan express a philosophy, make a sharp point or intrude in any way upon his tales unless it is to chuckle in sympathy at the ironies needed to hold together any true chronicles of human folly. His words are not cathedrals. You won't find flying buttresses in his cadences or Gothic transepts in his descriptions. Rather you will find a country church, newly whitewashed and as plain as the cornfields or faith. He is a craftsman who prefers an honest simplicity or a shaker chair over a cardinal's throne. And the stories, fiction or true, are very good.

BILL GRANGER

Introduction

Chicago, between the World's Columbian Exposition in 1893 and World War I, made a distinct, dominant and lasting impact on both American architecture and literature, a fact in which the city prides itself.

"The Chicagoization of America" attempts to establish that similar contributions were made by the Metropolis of the Midwest to the country's culture in other major areas of human endeavor.

These included:

- an updated, American language to help replace the King's English;
- a Chicago sponsorship of impressionists over the traditional art patronized elsewhere in the country as well as Chicago-trained artists who left a strong impression on the art world;
- a great era of penny journalism that brought in as readers even the people who lived in the back alley apartments;
- new experiments in education by Francis Parker and John Dewey;
- the social work ideas of Jane Addams and Hull House;
- the political notions of John Peter Altgeld and the Chicago Platform of 1896;
- urban reform by groups such as the Civic Federation and City Club;
- a new vision of the law according to Clarence Darrow;
- the hopes of Eugene Debs to organize the non-skilled workers;
- the mail order ideas of Aaron Montgomery Ward and Richard Sears that catered to the less-affluent;
- the ethnic awareness of "The Jungle" and the convictions of

Ida B. Wells, Ferdinand Barnett and others toward racial equality.

The nation-stirring result was that the city's freshness and its sense of democracy became the country's. The vigorous ideas eminating from Chicago smothered for a time the East Coast's penchant for a more imitative and elitist culture.

The experiments of pre-World War I Chicago were bluntly ended by the propaganda and disillusionment of that conflict. In their idealistic forms, these efforts seemed to have dropped off the face of the earth, replaced by the cynicism, banality and gangsterism of the 1920s. In reality, they were very often absorbed into the American culture.

The years between 1893 and 1917 in Chicago had been an ideal time for idealists, a believing age for progressives and a some-what buried treasure for the readers. They would be followed by an era inundated by disillusionment and skepticism as the people seemed to doubt that Chicago's ideals and their own commitments had been real.

Contents

Part I

Introduction to an Evolution

Part II

The Word and the Line Are Changed

Part III
From New Forms, New Freedoms

Part IV
Epilogue: An End and a Beginning

Part I

Introduction to an Evolution

The distinction between a revolution and an evolution is often the difference between a sword and a ploughshare. In 1776, the Colonies formally initiated their revolution. In 1893, the United States launched its most important evolution. The first was meant to make America a republic; the second, to turn it into a democracy. The American Revolution started on the East Coast and the evolution, in Chicago, Illinois.

Chicago, a City and an Idea

Back in 1893, Chicago was America's second largest city and its biggest idea.

Previously, the United States had proven that its republican form of government could work in the New England villages and the frontier towns of the west. In the large cities, however, the country had reverted to a class society imitating the social customs, culture and elitism of Europe to make certain that at least the "better" people would survive and their children prosper.

New York, for example, was in its "gilded age," a term popularized as the title of a chaotic novel of that name written by Mark Twain and Charles Dudley Warner in 1873. New York's socially elite "400" dominated the city's taste, finances, art, architecture, business and politics. Of them, Ward McAllister had said in 1888, "If you go out of that number you strike people who are either not at ease in a ballroom or else make other people not at ease." In contrast, 14,000 children were turned away from the public schools in New York in 1889 because there were not enough classrooms. Similarly, the pride of Boston and Philadelphia was not their citizens but their "upper crusts."

Chicago, on the other hand, was common. It had few pretensions. The town stank of stockyards that were the largest in the world and was covered with soot as befitted the railroad capital of the nation.

Historians Lloyd Lewis and Henry Justin Smith called Chicago of the 1880s "loud, frank and unsystematic."

British author Rudyard Kipling in that decade wrote of Chicago: "This place is the first American city I have encountered. Having seen it I urgently desire never to see it again. It is inhabited by savages."1

Kipling notwithstanding, there was hope in the East that missionary outposts of classical culture could be established. Even in

Chicago there might be a prep school, a literary club or even a grandiose neo-classical building. Around them, those natives could flock who had discriminating tastes, pedigree or wealth. Thus they could survive in this culturally-barren Midwest.

Then, like a Klondike, Chicago happened.

Chicago had become big, an international sensation. In the year 1800, Indians populated the place known as Chicagou. By the 1890s the city had turned into an international magnet of western peoples and had acquired a population of more than one million.[2] It was close on the heels of New York to becoming the largest city in the United States.

Chicago had become the most famous place in the world to go: if you had hope; if you wanted to reform other people or corrupt them; if you wished to make money or spend it; if you just desired to survive or chose to live recklessly; if you couldn't even write or if you hoped to be a writer; if you wanted to see America's streets paved with gold or were willing to trudge through dust or mud to go to work in the stockyards; or if you were running away, whether from the Tsar, conscription or the neo-slavery of the South.

Many feared these immigrants and migrants no matter where they came from and predicted only chaos for Chicago. Many of the literate and wealthy boastfully said that Chicago would see some cultural growth despite what was happening. No one foresaw that, with a startling suddenness, Chicago would become the motherlode of a rich, new American culture not beholden to the established and the wealthy, as had every other prosperous culture in history.

Two books written by the late Hugh Duncan show in depth Chicago's intellectual contribution to the American culture during this period. Unfortunately, his works did not get the recognition or distribution they deserved. Duncan's books are "The Rise of Chicago as a Literary Center from 1885 to 1920" (Bedminster Press, 1964), and "Culture and Democracy" (Bedminster Press, 1965). The latter is subtitled, "The struggle for form in society and architecture in Chicago and the Middle West during the life and times of Louis H. Sullivan." His works are scarce and treasured by scholars on Chicago. In his preface to "Culture and Democracy," he wrote perhaps more hopefully than factually, "The intellectual contributions of the Middle West are beginning to be recognized."

In many ways, the Chicago of that generation has become as separated from the rest of the world as is the fabled Atlantis, buried not under the sea, but under a lost sense of democracy and the 1920s ratatat image of the city's gangsters. But, unlike Atlantis, we can trace Chicago's lasting impact on American history, lifestyle and culture.

That Chicago has not been lost. It diffused into America. To return historically to the Chicago of that era is to experience much of America at its noblest, at its most sensual and in its innate purpose.[3]

The unamalgamated poor of Chicago took their pennies and discriminatingly patronized a new kind of writing that was so authentic and powerful that the city became—according to the high priest of American letters, H.L. Mencken—"the literary capital of the United States."

In the sanctum of literature and the even more inner one of architecture, the people of Chicago forged a newness that overrode the East's efforts to extend an elite culture to the expanding nation.

Simply put, the city of Chicago created modern architecture and saw the dominance of the "Chicago School" in the field. The "crowd," according to an insightful commentator, "created the skyscraper in Chicago." Louis Sullivan, meanwhile, wrestled with the establishment to show that designing buildings could become a great expression of democracy.

Whatever the area in which the city's voice was dominating, the word was that the town was working. It smelled awful and it was grimy. But—stinking and dirty—Chicago was the source of a vigorous, new American lifestyle. Much of the city's experience in this era would remain part of the American culture. Still, a group of Chicagoans—from John Peter Altgeld to Carl Sandburg—came to the surface and testified to even deeper and richer veins of democracy that have yet to be mined.

World War I then intervened and shelved some of these reports. The democracy Chicago had generated became the very slogan under which America entered that conflict. The city—reluctantly in some parts—was led into the fight by an Eastern college professor turned President, Woodrow Wilson.

The democratic institutions which peace had sown in the Midwest soil would be uprooted and replaced by the patriotic "virtues" of battle as the United States in 1917.

While the year is arbitrary, it coincides with the United States' entry into World War I, when Chicago became better at producing armament than ideas. It was not a war that Chicago welcomed very openly and its mayor Big Bill Thompson was often called "Kaiser Bill" for his lukewarm attitude toward it. Still, many of the city's social and intellectual thrusts had weakened well before 1917. A nation that set out to kill human beings could not really and deeply believe that goodness and power come from the people. As a result, the experiences of Chicago's great democrats would be pushed aside in the telling for those of the doughboys who had been in Flanders Fields, at Verdun or in the woods around Chateau Thierry.

The young Chicago was not an elitist city,[4] a hybrid tendril incapable of reproducing its life, but rather the town Carl Sandburg described in the poem, "Chicago," as:

> Laughing even as the ignorant fighter laughs
> who has never lost a battle,
> Bragging and laughing that under his
> wrist is the pulse and
> under his ribs the heart of the people,
> Laughing
> Laughing the stormy, husky, brawling
> laughter of Youth,
> Half-naked, sweating, proud to be Hog Butcher,
> Tool Maker, Stacker of Wheat, Player with
> Railroads and Freight Handler to the Nation.

Chicago: A City and an Idea

1. The actual title of Kipling's article was: "How I Struck Chicago and How Chicago Struck Me, of Religion, Politics, and Pig-sticking, and the Incarnation of the City Among the Shambles."

2. Chicago's non-Indian population grew in 100 years from one fur trader (Jean Baptiste Point DuSable, who sold out in the late 1790s) to almost 1.7 million in 1900 and more than 2 million by 1910.

3. Chicago in the book is not defined as stopping at the corporate limits. In his 1918 book, "The Valley of Democracy" (Scribners), Meredith Nicholson wrote: "Chicago not only draws strength from a vast territory but, through myriad agencies and avenues, sends back a mighty power from its huge dynamo." Of the city, he says, "The pilgrim who lands on the lake shore with an open mind and a fair understanding of what America is about—the unprejudiced traveler—is immediately conscious that here, indeed, is a veritable capital of democracy."

4. Lincoln Steffens' description of Chicago at the time is graphic, to say the least. In his book "The Shame of the Cities" (McClure, Phillips & Co., 1904), he called Chicago: "First in violence, deepest in dirt; loud, lawless, unlovely, ill-smelling, irreverent, new; an overgrown gawk of a village, the 'tough' among cities, a spectacle to the nation."

1893, New York's Beachhead along Chicago's Shoreline

In 1893 the eastern seaboard's neo-classical culture established a beachhead along Chicago's southeastern shoreline. It was known as the World's Columbian Exposition and relics still stand in the Jackson Park: a replica of the gilded statue of The Republic and the Palace of the Arts, the framework of which houses the Museum of Science and Industry. The fair was, however, a highwater mark of that attempted invasion, and the relics are as symbolic as the cannons left behind after Napoleon's retreat from Russia or the German tanks left rotting in the African desert since World War II.

Even to this day, Chicago remains deceived by the World's Columbian Exposition and proudly commemorates it with a star in the city's flag along with the Fort Dearborn Massacre, the Chicago Fire, and the 1933-34 A Century of Progress Exposition. To a large extent, Chicago did wring a victory out of the happening because people who came to see the White City, as the 1893 world's fair was known, found Chicago the far greater attraction.

The concept of the world's fair was to commemorate the 400th anniversary of Columbus's discovery of America. And, indeed, a number of aspects of the event, such as the visit of a descendant of Columbus, the presence of full-scale models of the Nina, Pinta and Santa Maria and the statue of Columbia did recognize the occasion. The World's Columbian Exposition, however, was to be a fair, a celebration, the likes of which never had been seen before and perhaps has not since.

The exposition itself, however, was very alien to the city that hosted it. Its message and Chicago's could not have been more distinctly different.

The very first image one had of the World's Columbian Exposition was that it was white, whitewashed white. In the days before bright fabrics, white was the color of the wealthy. They could afford it as well as the cleaning necessary to keep it so. Their clothes, linen, furniture, buildings, even their little picket fences were white. Those of the less affluent varied from gray to black.

White was not the color of Chicago.[1]

The major buildings of the World's Columbian Exposition were neo-classical with one exception, the Transportation Building, at that time was considered one of the lesser structures on the fair grounds. The appropriations for seven others were larger, with the cost of the Manufactures Building more than 4 1/2 times more.

The four major architectural firms that designed the grandiose buildings of the World's Columbian Exposition were from the East Coast: Richard M. Hunt of New York, Administration Building; Peabody and Stearns of Boston, Machinery Hall; McKim, Mead & White of New York, Agricultural Building; and George B. Post of New York, Manufactures and Liberal Arts.[2]

Ordinarily, it would have meant little where architects were from, except that the New York and Boston firms represented a radically different school of architecture than did those in Chicago such as Adler and Sullivan, Jenny and Mundie, S. S. Beman and Henry Ives Cobb. Members of the Chicago school of architecture were building the world's first skyscrapers, lean structures functionally designed to rest on steel skeletons. Generally, they had little room for bowing to the classical architecture typical of New York.

With the exception of Louis Sullivan, even the Chicago architects, however, knuckled under in building the World's Columbian Exposition. They were clearly told to go along and they did.

Not only were the major architectural firms from New York, but also three key figures in designing the fair were from there. Architect Frederick Law Olmstead, the New York landscape artist best known for designing Central Park in Manhattan, laid out the grounds. The major sculptor and the artist's artist in the planning of the exposition was Augustus Saint-Gaudens, from the state of New York. He chose many of the other sculptors and painters.[3] Finally, Charles B. Atwood, of New York was Designer in Chief and did most of the designing: 60 buildings in all.

In all of this New Yorkness to the World's Columbian Exposition, there was a deliberate plan. It existed in the mind and intention of the man who had been given the power to construct the World's Columbian Exposition. He was a Chicagoan, and his name was Daniel Burnham.

Simply put, Burnham thought that New York's culture was "surpassing" to Chicago's.

Burnham was not so much an architect as an administrator and an ingratiator. He was a dreamer, but his dreams were colored by the pressure of regularly dealing in rich men's dreams. His first major architectural commission with his partner, John Root, was to build a mansion for a wealthy man, the daughter of whom he subsequently married.

The city of New York was only slightly less appreciative of Daniel Burnham than he of it for his letting New York build its world's fair in Chicago. On March 25, 1893, a month before the opening of the exposition and two years after the major work had begun, New York held a banquet in its Madison Concert Hall to thank Chicagoan Daniel Burnham and to present him with a loving cup. Daniel Burnham, we are told, accepted the gratitude with "blushes."[4]

Chicago originally had fought hard to have the fair, and New York was at first embittered about losing out.[5]

What made the World's Columbian Exposition so very important was the railroads. Suddenly, because of them, the average family could easily travel hundreds of miles to come. Such mobility was new and astonishing. Only wars or famines had ever caused movements of people on such a scale before.

So great was the pull of the exposition in Jackson Park that people spent their burial money or sold the family horse to go.

Four major United States cities had wanted it: New York, Washington D.C., St. Louis and Chicago. All pledged millions of dollars to support it. Ultimately, the decision for the site went to Congress, and in perhaps the liveliest political confrontation of 1889, Chicago won.

In the final stages of the debate, the other cities seemed to unite so that any city except Chicago would win. Chicago finally won out on the eighth roll call in the House. The choice was confirmed 43 to 13 in the Senate.

Kenny Williams, in her book, "In the City of Men," reports that the opposition to Chicago was based in the opponents' belief that "Chicago was not the city to invite the scrutiny of the world." It was an issue of "dignity." One senator pointed out that if he had to vote between Chicago and Hades as the site, he would be strictly neutral.

One perhaps can understand a little that his inferiority complex about Chicago drove Daniel Burnham to import New York's culture for the world's fair. Such motivation, however, only did further damage because it was shared by other elitist Chicagoans.

The World's Columbian Exposition was designed to have a deep cultural impact on the nation, and it did. It came at a time when this country was groping its way out of profound sectionalism and parochialism. The railroads, mass transit, the telephone and the telegraph were uniting the United States. In so doing, a void of a common culture, language, arts, religion and literature was becoming apparent. Congresses in each of these areas were held in connection with the World's Columbian Exposition. For example, there were gatherings of authors, inventors, painters and architects. And the first International Congress of Religion ever was held at the exposition.

To a large extent, however, architecture was the most focused facet of culture with which the fair dealt. It was the stage upon which all other aspects were examined. Realism in literature, for example, was one of the debates of the day, but the discussion itself could only be so real in the neo-classical surroundings of the exposition.

Furthermore, the sumptuousness and the whiteness of the architecture was meant to overawe rather than to involve the visitors in the event. Burnham saw it as "molding and directing the higher purposes of American life." The Midway with its hoochie-coochie dancers and the Ferris Wheel as well as Chicago itself were apparently disdainfully tolerated by the elite to deal with lower purposes.[6]

In actual gate count, the World's Columbian Exposition had 27 million visitors, 21 million of whom paid to get in. In contrast, the presidential vote in the whole country the year before was under 12 million. In 1893, the United States had a population of approximately 66 million.

The higher the gate count, the more it concerned a Chicagoan and an architect, the one man who saw incisively the potential damage of the World's Columbian Exposition. He was Louis Sullivan.

Sullivan felt that art and architecture should be a function of life and not an escape from it. He saw the form of the World's Columbian Exposition as embodying the notion of running away from life and Chicago as representing embracing it.

His words about the exposition in which he participated, designing the Transportation Building, were impassioned. Sullivan criticized not so much a school of architecture as a lifestyle and a philosophy of life. He called the neo-classical approach that was represented in the architecture, sculpture, painting and culture of the fair as "feudal". He meant the word in contrast to democratic. He saw it representing some preconceived struggle of good and evil rather than the experimental expression of the good, which he sought.

Louis Sullivan's commentary on the World's Columbian Exposition is almost too compact to comprehend. His words seem to rush ahead of his ideas, but they are worth pursuing.[7]

Summing up "the educational and moral value of the exposition" in one of the closing speeches, fair director Selim Hobart Peabody pointed with pride to the relationship between values and the architecture of the exhibition.

Peabody said:

> The lessons that most impressed the millions who visited the wonders of the exposition, which they accepted with greatest unanimity, and which they will gladly recall as memory reproduces the events and the scenes of their pilgrimage, were those taught by the achievements of the landscape artist and the architect.

In "The Autobiography of an Idea," Louis Sullivan was greatly worried about those lessons:

> The damage wrought by the World's Fair will last for half a century from its date, if not longer. It has penetrated deep into the constitution of the American mind, effecting there lesions significant of dementia.[8]

Sullivan was not simply a man of words but also an architect of revolutionary inventiveness. Burnham had to be talked into letting Sullivan design the Transportation Building, "the structure from which modern architecture as a movement is generally considered to have sprung," according to Claude Bragdon in his introduction to Sullivan's 1924 book.

By way of contrast, we have Sullivan's description of the exposition itself:

> The work completed, the gates thrown open May 1, 1893, the crowds flowed in from every quarter,

continued to flow throughout a fair-weather summer and a serenely beautiful October. Then came the end. The gates closed.

These crowds were astonished. They beheld what was for them an amazing revelation of the architectural art, of which previously they in comparison had known nothing. To them it was a veritable Apocalypse, a message inspired from on high. Upon it their imagination shaped new ideals. They went away, spreading again over the land, returning to their homes, each one of them carrying in the soul the shadow of the white cloud, each of them permeated by the most subtle and slow acting of poisons: an imperceptible miasma within the shadow of a higher culture. A vast multitude, exposed, unprepared, they had not time nor occasion to become immune to forms of sophistication not their own, to a higher and more dexterously insidious plausibility. Thus they departed joyously carriers of contagion, unaware that what they had beheld and believed to be truth was to prove, in historic fact, an appalling calamity. For what they saw was not all they believed they saw, but an imposition of the spurious upon their eyesight, a naked exibitionism of charlatanry in the higher feudal and domineering culture, conjoined with expert salesmanship of the materials of decay.9

Sullivan pointed out in retrospect that the virus of the exposition gave this nation,

Tudor for colleges and residences: Roman for banks and railway stations and libraries, or Greek if you like some customers prefer the Ionic to the Doric. We have French, English and Gothic, Classic and Renaissance for churches.10

In retrospect, we still have very little feeling how far from reality the architecture of such institutions has led us. But, as one goes into county seat after county seat in America, and sees those monstrosities of past architecture serving as county court houses, one can get an inkling of what false notions of dignity we have stuck on to the administration of justice in this land. Or, when one sees the Gothic or Romanesque churches, one wonders how much that has redefined the notion of prayer. Or, how esoteric has the architecture of nation's libraries, museums and theater made art and literature. How much has our nation's true culture been diluted by the imitation and import that came out of the World's Columbian Exposition?

Fortunately, the World's Columbian Exposition made only a beachhead in Chicago. When it closed in late 1893, the more democratic forces of Chicago were unleased once more and Porkopolis, as it was deridingly known, began to make some beachheads of its own in this land.[11]

1. A number of writers played on the theme of the fair being the White City; and Chicago, covered with railroad soot, the Black City. One was Paul Bourget, who wrote "Farewell to the White City" in *Cosmopolitan Magazine* (December, 1893). He saw the White City as "promise," even though he spoke of the "black city, which will endure forever."

2. Small photos tend to distort the impact of the Columbian Exposition because its size and accurate scale were so integral to the classical conception of it. The Greek Peristyle, Italian Renaissance Court of Honor and the major buildings were massive. The smaller buildings were described as "palaces." The idea seemed to be to create, by every means, a sense of awe.

3. Among the sculptors were: Daniel French, who created the famous Republic statue; Frederick MacMonnies, who designed the fair's major fountain; Edwin Kemys, remembered as the dentist who designed the lions in front of Chicago's Art Institute; Saint-Gauden's brother, Louis, and Loredo Taft, who was to become identified with several of Chicago's best known sculptures, notably the "Fountain of Time," in Washington Park, and "Death," in Graceland Cemetery.

4. Charles Moore's two-volume biography of Daniel Burnham devotes a full chapter to "The New York Dinner" and describes it as "lionizing a Daniel." The highest praise on the occasion came from Professor Charles Eliot Norton of Harvard, who "reputedly admired nothing modern, not even modern man."

5. It was at this time that Chicago acquired its nickname "The Windy City." Charles Dana in an editorial in the *New York Sun* warned his readers to pay no attention "to the claims of that windy city. Its people could not build a world's fair even if it won it."

6. For a description of the human side of the fair, see "Chicago, the History of its Reputation" by Chicago historians Lloyd Lewis and Henry Justin Smith (Hartcourt, Brace amd Company, 1929) p.189-215. 1893 was a Depression year, and free passes were the best many Chicagoans could hope for.

7. Louis Sullivan's evaluation of the Columbian Exposition was published as part of "The Autobiography of an Idea." It first appeared in print in 1924. An even fuller appreciation of his positive ideas about architecture comes through in the pages of "Kindergarten Chats," originally a series of articles published in 1901 in the magazine *The Interstate Architect and Builder.*

8. "The Autobiography of an Idea" (Press of the American Institute of Architecture, 1924) p.325.

9. Ibid. p.321.

10. Ibid. p.326.

11. Chicago novelist Henry Blake Fuller saw the end of the world's fair as the "city's graduation day," but like many others he hoped for and saw the city nudging its way gently in among the nation's "cultured" aristocrats.

The People of Chicago, Yes

Chicago in the 20 years after the World's Columbian Exposition is remembered for its ideas, events and its leaders, but even more for people, a whole generation of them. They were thrown together from a world of different places and in very great numbers. In their struggle and survival they created strong democratic forces that long would affect the whole country.

The city of Chicago was the vortex of the country's melting pot. One could look into it and see all the ingredients swirling around and around.

Many writers did just that. They sat on the rim, looked in and recorded what or rather whom they saw. Such reporting—when it was faithful—had little trouble becoming great literature.

The word portraits and pictures they left for Chicago are far more valuable than the treasures closely guarded in the Art Institute of Chicago or the mansions along the North Shore. For these are the first people who ever created a national culture that broke enough with elitist and aristocratic values to be called democratic.

Theodore Dreiser, for example, wrote about both the rich and the poor of Chicago in such books as "Sister Carrie," "The Titan" and "The Financier." Finley Peter Dunne captured something of the soul of Chicago's South Side Irish in his character Mr. Dooley. Edna Ferber and Willa Cather wrote about the city's simple people. Frank Norris wrote about the city's traders in grain futures in "The Pit." Henry Blake Fuller and Joseph Medill Patterson frequently wrote about people who were Chicago-born.

The people, however, who will be remembered the longest from this era were the immigrants, simply because there were so very many of them, hundreds of thousands. These new Chicagoans were pictured poignantly and "immortalized" as characters in 1906 in a novel, "The Jungle," Upton Sinclair's expose about Chicago's stockyards.[1] "The Jungle," despite its oppressive title and plot, remains probably the most panoramic photograph ever taken of Chicago.

Jurgis[2] Rudkus is the novel's hero, a strong Lithuanian immigrant who must exchange his golden dreams for a survival plan; his self-confidence, for a hope for a better day.

Jurgis and other immigrants were forced to realize that in Chicago they never could survive by themselves, only by being helped and by helping others.

"The Jungle" meticulously unravels how painful was the transition for those dreamers who came to Chicago and to its streets reportedly paved with riches. One character in the book, Grandmother Majauszkiene, was the embodiment of the wise turn-of-the-century immigrant to Chicago and all the pressure and pain such people saw. Of her, author Upton Sinclair wrote:

> Grandmother Majauszkiene had come to America with her son at a time when so far as she knew there was only one other Lithuanian family in the district. The workers had all been Germans then, skilled cattle-butchers that the packers had brought from abroad to start the business.
>
> Afterward, as cheaper labor had come, these Germans moved away.
>
> The next were the Irish. There had been six or eight years when Packingtown had been a regular Irish city. There were a few colonies of them still here, enough to run all the unions and the police force and get all the graft. But most of those who were working in the packinghouses had gone away after the next drop in wages—after the big strike.
>
> The Bohemians had come then, and after them the Poles. People said that old man Durham (the owner) himself was responsible for these immigrations. He had sworn that he would fix the people of Packingtown so that they would never call a strike again on him, and so he sent his agents into every city and village in Europe to spread the tale of the chances of

> work and high wages at the stockyards.
>
> The people had come in hordes, and old Durham had squeezed them tighter and tighter, speeding them up and grinding them to pieces and sending for new ones.
>
> The Poles, who had come by the tens of thousands, had been driven to the wall by the Lithuanians, and now the Lithuanians were giving way to the Slovaks. Who there was poorer and more miserable than the Slovaks, Grandmother Majauszkiene had no idea, but the packers would find them, never fear.[3]

The meatpackers were only one of many groups who found ways to use the people of Chicago, especially the immigrants, for their own gains. George Pullman, whom even the socially conservative Eugene Field mocked as the "Markeesy di Pullman," represented "enlightened" factory owners who found ways to lower the cost of labor. Department stores using child labor and the city's sweatshops helped merchants make fabulous fortunes.

The most powerful expose of conditions under which Chicagoans were forced to live during the 1890s appeared in the book "If Christ Came to Chicago," written by William T. Stead in 1894.[4]

The English journalist named names and pulled the crowns of Chicago's mighty down over their ears for their callousness.[5]

George Pullman, he excoriated as "like a mediatized sovereign in Germany" who did not hesitate to make 600 percent profit off the natural gas he sold his workers to light their homes. Marshall Field, he rated little better for seeking sweatshop goods from out of state when Illinois finally banned sweatshops. Stead remonstrated them along with Philip D. Armour as "The Chicagoan Trinity."

Of Armour, Stead wrote:

> In thinking of Mr. Armour, as of Mr. Field, even when we contemplate the lavish generosity with which he endows an institution which bares his name, it is difficult to forget the ruin of the small tradesmen. Mr. Armour feels no compunction, say in conducting a campaign against the butchers of Joliet...where by the aid of preferential railway rates and his enormous

> wealth he is able to drive into the bankruptcy courts the tradesmen who refuse to deal with Armour.[6]

Stead had little trouble finding others at whom to point the accusatory finger of injustice. The railroads not only paid low wages and fought unionization but also created a cruel trap for Chicagoans by refusing to elevate railroad crossings throughout the city. Using bribery, for many years they fought the attempt to force them to do it through city ordinance. The situation, by comparison, is hardly imaginable today. Stead did not hold back in his graphic description of it in 1894:

> Instead of bridging her railroads or making them bridge her streets, Chicago has avoided bridge making wherever possible and allowed the railroads to run along and across the public thoroughfares of a crowded city at the street level.
>
> If a stranger's first impression of Chicago is that of the barbarous gridironed streets, his second is that of the multitude of mutilated people whom he sees on crutches. Excepting immediately after a great war, I have never seen so many mutilated fragments of humanity as one finds in Chicago. Dealers in artificial limbs and crutches ought to be able to do a better business in Chicago than in any other city I have ever visited. On inquiry I found that the second salient feature of Chicago was a direct result of the first. The railroads which cross the city at the level in every direction, although limited by statute and ordinance as to speed, constantly mow down unoffending citizens at the crossings, and those legless, armless men and women whom you meet on the streets are merely the mangled remnant of the massacre that is constantly going on year in and year out.
>
> "Can nothing be done?" you ask in amazement, and you are told the mayor is trying do something but that it is very doubtful if he can succeed, the railroad corporations are so powerful. "But what about those infamous street car tracks with their murderous flanges?

> Can nothing be done to substitute more civilized tracks?" Another shake of the head, a shrug of the shoulders. "Ask Baron [Charles T.] Yerkes! He owns Chicago." The corporations have stolen everything. The citizens have not even a miserable revenue from the franchise which gave the corporations their power. It did not begin all at once, this usurpation, but now it is complete.[7]

It was not always the corporation or powerful business tycoons, however, who preyed upon the poor, the immigrant or the average citizen. Street crime, for example, was a very real Chicago commodity at the turn-of-the-century.[8] In the 1890s, for instance, the owner of the Lone Star Saloon and Palm Garden, "a low dive," named a drink after himself, "The Mickey Finn Special."[9] It was laced probably with chloral hydrate, was advertised prominently above the bar and could put a person into a deep sleep until its effects wore off.

While the drug was doing its work, Mickey Finn and his accomplices not only robbed the victim but also substituted rags for any decent items of clothing he happened to be wearing.

The knockout drink was one of many tricks that bar and brothel owners used to fleece the unwary. Finn's establishment probably got the "stiffest" punishment of any, however. In 1909, after five years of serving "The Mickey Finn Special," the saloon had its license revoked.

An even more tragic fate than a knockout drop often awaited the immigrant who arrived, as almost all did, at the Harrison Street train station. The coterie of vicious humans who waited in the wings there varied from bag snatchers[10] to con men (using the languages of the immigrants) and pimps ready to pull unsuspecting young women into the city's web of prostitution. New York faced the same problem and eventually solved it by hermetically sealing off the immigrants until they boarded their trains, very often headed for Chicago.[11]

Once past the bag and body snatchers at Harrison Street Station, immigrants found there were few jobs, addresses of relatives were very often vague and often there was not even a place to stay. Hunger competed with the language barrier as the number one problem facing them, not only immediately, but also in many cases for years.

In the worst of times the jails housed and the saloon owners fed the needy. Many were "lucky" to be sent along with the insane to the county work farm at Dunning.[12]

Health needs in the city fared little better. The packinghouses were anything but sanitary, and those who ate the meat prepared there too often regretted it. The newspapers daily carried a map of the city with little black and white flags indicating the sections of the city where the water had to be boiled that day because of the danger of typhoid fever. Even with a white flag, people took their chances.

For the poor or average citizen there were no doctors,[13] except to sign death certificates. Medicine came from the cabinet stocked when the patent medicine man came around the neighborhood or by cut-rate cure-alls from the mail order houses.

And yet this was the Chicago that hundreds of thousands people came from across an ocean to become part of. Why? Because of a dream and because existence where they had been had become impossible. But, more important, why did they stay? They didn't in the Klondike or the mining towns of the West. In Chicago, however, they found they could survive and build at least a part of their dream, or their children would be able to do so.

First, however, came survival and the scars of that struggle 100 years ago are still apparent in Chicago today. No matter how much of a haven Chicago supplied, there was always an insecurity, a job that had to be held onto fiercely, a house that had to be protected from the man who had sold it on land contract. There were children who so strenuously needed providing for that a parent often didn't have time for them. The fall-back position for immigrants was their religion, for it promised heaven after the struggle was over.

Future generations would look back and not understand the scars and the self-imposed limits on individual freedom that people accepted to survive. Worse, their children and future offspring would not appreciate the great things that the turn-of-the-century Chicago immigrants achieved under fantastic pressure.

It was the poor who chose democracy. They did not want to go to a dictatorial form of government to solve even their most immediate and dramatic problems. They did not seek out the European model of a class society as did the East Coast and many of the wealthy of the country. The immigrant and the man on the street often had a concept of democracy that might appear simplistic but which had all the merits of being simple and as much worth struggling for as job or home.

Pullman's workers, for example, rebelled against him, and other railroad workers joined in the 1894 strike in the Pullman area of Chicago even though it meant hunger and loss of their jobs and homes.

The "people" of Chicago opted for democracy in the newspapers and in the writers they chose. There was a stable of writers ready for their patronage, ones who chose to imitate the more aloof style of New York and Boston. The people chose instead Eugene Field, George Ade, Finley Peter Dunne, Theodore Dreiser, Upton Sinclair, Willa Cather, Vachel Lindsay, Ben Hecht and Carl Sandburg. The newspapers themselves by the middle 1890s had begun to understand better where the people were and let them shape Chicago journalism.

Chicagoans—many of them—clutched their votes tightly. Precinct captains seemed easily able to inveigle votes from immigrants for a sandwich, a job or a half dollar, only to find that not they but the reformers had those votes the next election. The reformers thereupon found that their aristocratic form of democracy could not take root in Chicago and themselves lost the voters.

Meanwhile, the governments chosen by Chicago came up with solutions to even the toughest problems that the mushrooming city could present. The surface line tracks were elevated, Yerkes was defeated in the City Council showdown and the Chicago River was effectively reversed in 1900. Instead of emptying into Lake Michigan, the river now flowed into the Sanitary and Ship Canal, down the Illinois River to the Mississippi, the water purifying itself as it moved. It ended the typhoid problem.

The essential ingredients that Chicagoans lent to democracy were the choices that they made. Historically, there is a tendency to place too much emphasis on the votes people did or did not cast and not to look at the full flush decisions they were making.

Carl Sandburg wrote a lengthy volume of free verse with the title, "The People, Yes."[14] It is an affirmation of democracy in the broadest and truly Chicago sense by a man who spent most of his years studying Abraham Lincoln, Chicago and the people. The three subjects are very much related.

The words "The People, Yes" are probably the most succinct statement of Chicago's message. Sandburg's ideas about "The People" helped to clarify the phrase's meaning.

Sandburg wrote:

The people is everyman, everybody.
Everybody is you and me and all others.15

In quoting Abraham Lincoln elsewhere in the book, Sandburg got to the essence of democracy:

> As I would not be a slave, so I would not be a master. This expresses my idea of democracy... Whatever differs from this, to the extent of the difference, is no democracy.

Many people believe in democracy without experiencing it. The Chicagoans of the 1890s and early 1900s had many opportunities to experience and grow in it. The landed people in the early days of America had a republic that excluded the participation of slaves, women and often those who did not hold property. The small towns had government of the people, but it was easier to see equality there. In Chicago, in the 1890s, women and blacks were far from attaining their democratic rights but were more clearly demanding them than elsewhere. The main group that was suddenly attaining freedom, however, was the landless and the immigrant. It was a new experience for those from Europe or even from the Chicago of the 1880s, in which many class distinctions had been an accepted part of the city's lifestyle.

Those who in their souls were aristocratic openly ridiculed the people for their supposed lack of taste, their seeming willingness to be fooled, their reputed lack of political concern and their presumed stupidity. Those who mock are never able to understand why their own eloquence and ideas flourish and then die as though they lacked roots.

Why? Because as Sandburg wrote:

The people live on.
The learning and blundering people
will live on.
They will be tricked and again sold
And go back to the nourishing earth
for rootholds...16

The People of Chicago, Yes

In the 1890s in Chicago, the people did a lot of breaking loose. And the more they broke loose, the more they became free, the more they became a democracy. And that experience, in Chicago for one generation at the turn-of-the-century, became better than any definition, no matter how poetic, of the word "people."

1. The strongest immediate impact of "The Jungle," to the disappointment of Upton Sinclair, was on pure food legislation rather than on wages and working conditions of packinghouse workers. He had incidentally described a few practices arguably "common" to the packers, grinding up rats with other meat, using hogs that had died of cholera to make fancy brand lard, and accepting steers that were tubercular. President Theodore Roosevelt read the book and was not a little upset. Finley Peter Dunne, a Chicago newspaper wit who had burst upon the national scene, had his character, Irish-brogued Mr. Dooley, describe the Rooseveltian reaction in an often-quoted passage from "Mr. Dooley on Ivrything and Ivrybody" (Dover, 1963) p.237:

> Tiddy was toying with a light breakfast an' idly turnin' over th' pages iv th' new book with both hands. Suddenly he rose fr'm th' table, an' cryin', "I'm pizened," begun throwin' sausages out iv th' window. Th' ninth wan sthruck Sinitor Biv'ridge on th' head an' made a blond. It bounced off, exploded, an' blew a leg off a secret-service agent, an' th' scatthred fragmints destroyed a handsome row iv ol' oak-trees. Sinitor Biv'ridge rushed in, thinkin' that th' Presidint was bein' assassynated be his devoted followers in th' Sinit, an' discovered Tiddy engaged in a hand-to-hand conflict with a potted ham. Th' Sinitor from Injyanny, with a few well-directed wurruds, put out fuse an' rendered th' missile harmless. Since thin th' Prisidint, like th' rest iv us, has become a viggytaryan.

2. Roosevelt did act as a result of "The Jungle." He sent two investigators to verify the facts and started a strong push that led to pure food laws. Sinclair's comment was, "I aimed at the public's heart and hit it in the stomach."

3. Pronounced "Yoorghis," it is the Lithuanian form of George.

4. The Signature Classic edition, p.71. The group in the next generation was to be blacks, although Poles, Lithuanians, Germans, Croatians and Italians continued to work in the stockyards in large numbers. By 1923, 24 percent of the workers for the two largest packers were blacks. Their introduction, as that of other groups before them, helped to ward off unionization by other than craft and company unions. Finally, in 1935 the CIO began an organizing drive in the packing industry that included the blacks as equals and which appealed enough to them so the company unions were finally broken 70 years after the founding of the Union Stock Yards. The story of blacks in the packinghouses and the struggle for unionization is told on p.302-311 in "Black Metropolis," by St. Clair Drake and Horace Clayton (Harcourt, Brace and Co., 1945).

5. This book by Stead was published early in 1894, before the Pullman Strike of that year. He later wrote "Chicago Today or the Labour War in America" (*Review of Reviews*, London, 1894), which is rarer even than original copies of his "If Christ Came To Chicago." In the former, he pointed out that George Pullman was worth $30 million (in capital) and owned 2,000 sleepers plus the city of Pullman at the time of the strike, when the issue was a cut-back in wages without any lowering of rent for his employees.

6. The following references are all from the chapter titled, "The Chicagoan Trinity" in "If Christ Came to Chicago" (Laird & Lee, 1894) p.84.

7. Ibid. p.187.

8. Dozens of books have been written on the history of crime in Chicago. The one that probably comes closest to being a classic is "Gem of the Prairie," by Herbert Asbury (Alfred A. Knopf, 1940). It gives an ample description (p.171-6) of the life and techniques of Chicagoan Mickey Finn.

9. Mickey Finn franchised his formula, but the terms "Mickey Finn" or simply "slip him a Mickey" came to mean the use of any kind of knockout drops.

10. Bag snatchers were active in Chicago terminals as early as 1854 and were cited as one of the reasons for the formation in the city of the German Aid Society in that year.

11. Chicago still differed from New York in handling immigrants at the tail end of the heavy immigration in 1923, according to a *Chicago Evening American* article of July 7 that year.

12. The "institutions" at Dunning included: the Poor House, the Hospital for Consumptives, the Hospital for the Insane and the Farm. Both the poor and the "chronic insane" worked not only on the farm but also on construction and in special "industries" to support the place. The man who held the title "The Farmer" had a prize political position. In 1989 the unmarked graves of hundreds of residents were uncovered in the commercial developement of a subdivision there.

13. Robert J. Casey in "Chicago Medium Rare" (Bobbs-Merrill Co., 1949) p.117 wrote humorously, graphically and nostalgically of the health hazards and cures in turn-of-the-century Chicago. His remembered remedy for croup:

> (A) Sleep with your window closed and avoid the night air.
>
> (B) Eat nothing but good, easily digested food such as oatmeal gruel.
>
> (C) Wear a copper finger ring to absorb the poisons.
>
> (D) Take a daily dose of sulfur and molasses.

14. "The People, Yes" was published in 1936 by Harcourt, Brace and World, Inc. Fifteen years later, Sandburg's compilation, "Complete Poems,"

won the 1951 Pulitzer Prize.

15. The quote from "The People, Yes" starts on p.14.
16. Ibid. pg. 107

The Town Almost Everyone Wanted to Reform

Chicago, at the turn-of-the-century, imported reformers but exported sensuality. Sitting on the shore of the undulating lake, the city chose to be naked and raw rather than be clothed in the respectability of something it was not.

That fact caused a hard lump in the throat of the reformers as well at times as, tears in their eyes, especially those standing in their pulpits.

Chicago, they recognized, was the source of a growing sensuality in the United States.

And, in the words of the song, it became the town even Billy Sunday could not shut down.

Chicago had a red light in its window with large sections openly catering to "the sins of the flesh." Chicago-style bordellos were imitated in almost every cowpoke town that had sprung up in the West. They very often copied the names of this city's more infamous brothels such as the "Carrie Nation's," "House of All Nations," "The Why Not" and later the "Everleigh Club."

More subtly, the Midwestern metropolis offered to the nation a sensuality that simply and directly said, "Hurrah for the senses and for things and people sensual."[1]

Such values left the city's reformers aghast no less than did its reputation for open vice. They were against an educational system spawned here (progressive, heaven forbid) in which the senses were given freedom in contrast to the traditional "proper respect" for cold intellectulalism and for rote memorizing. In art, they were revolted by Chicago's affair with the French impressionists. In architecture, to them, if emotion were to guide the pen, it had to be a long dead passion from the past of Rome, Greece or the 13th century France. The feelings of the poor—especially their emotional cries for justice—were to the reformers far secondary to the people's need for a retrenchment in morals, customs and thinking.[2]

The would-be changers—as is well known about Chicago—were never completely successful in altering its ways.

They were, however, distracting and did succeed at times in diverting some of the city's attention and strength as well as modifying, occasionally, its behavior.

Chicago's desire not to be reformed, to be itself, has been best exemplified by the men it has chosen for mayor. Reform candidates, especially ones who came at the city intellectually or with even a small amount of aloofness, simply never received the votes.

The mayor who perhaps best represented Chicago was the man the city especially chose in 1893 to be its host for the World's Columbian Exposition. He was Carter Harrison I, a man who loved to be among the people of Chicago, even to the extent of being physically present for such a potentially explosive event as the Haymarket speeches.[3] His doing so ultimately brought him so much vituperation in the aftermath of the Haymarket "riot" that he was considered politically dead. Seven years later, however, Chicago brought Carter Harrison back to be its mayor for the world's fair. Chicagoans believed he had "class" and style despite the protests of reformers that he didn't crack down on vice.

As a result, visitors found Chicago very much an open city. As one Marion, Indiana, citizen commented in words that have often been quoted:

> If Old Carter Harrison's elected mayor, I'm going to Chicago to the fair, but I'm going to wear nothing but tights and carry a knife between my teeth and a pistol in each hand.

In the matter of eloquence, Chicago was not to be disappointed in its mayor. On the last night of the fair, he addressed a meeting of mayors and said of Chicago:

> The young city is not only vigorous but she laves her beautiful limbs daily in Lake Michigan and comes out clean and pure every morning.

His words portrayed warm insight into Chicago's sensuality. Unfortunately, they were some of his last. That night he was shot and killed by a demented man who thought Harrison should have appointed him corporation counsel of Chicago. Others, from various angles, professions and viewpoints, have also tried to put into words a description of Chicago's rawness, nakedness, sensuality and ultimately, strength.

Theodore Dreiser, remembering his newspaper days in Chicago during the 1890s, said of it:

> It is given to some cities and to some lands to suggest romance and to me Chicago did that hourly. It sang, I thought, and in spite of what I deemed my various troubles, I was singing with it...Chicago was so young, so blithe, so new, I thought. Florence in its best days must have been something like this to young Florentines or Venice to young Venetians.

Such a person was hardly bent on reforming Chicago, although his novels did expose the powerful social evils of men like transit magnate Charles T. Yerkes.

A Chicagoan very clearly not in favor of reforming anything was one of its all time anti-heroes, Capt. George Wellington Streeter, a gun-runner, whose boat, The Reutan, sank in the sands off Chicago's abandoned Near North Side shoreline. He lived in the beached boat and as the sand filled in around it he claimed squatter's rights, proclaiming the area, "The District of Lake Michigan." More appropriately, as other reprobates joined him, it could have been called the "Red Light District of Lake Michigan."

Of Chicago, Capt. Streeter said, "A church and the WCTU (Woman's Christian Temperance Union) never growed a big town yet. Chicago, hit's still a frontier town."[4]

Fifty years later, a raucous Chicago alderman by the name of Paddy Bauler renewed Chicago's reprobate trademark with the comment, "Chicago ain't ready for reform."

More sophisticated voices repeatedly were describing essentially the same soul trait. Mary Borden said:

> No one is ever ashamed of anything in Chicago. Everything is moving too quickly, everyone is too specialized and it is all too much fun. Each one, whether crook or politician or expert gunman is too

> good of his kind to be conscious of anything less positive and less exhilarating than his own power.5

Chicago was fun. It was the fun of the Midway and the Ferris Wheel, however, rather than the ecstatic joy of the grandiose architecture of the Peristyle or Arts Building of the World's Columbian Exposition.

Chicago's sensuality also meant open, blatant sexuality. That could not have been more explicitly stated than it was by the Vice Commission of Chicago in 1911 when it reported that an estimated 27,375,000 separate acts of prostitution had been committed in the city's red light district in the previous year.

While the same Vice Commission honed in on the great racism and sexism which were an integral part of open vice, especially in Chicago, it was also a busybody group. It snooped on young people in ice cream parlors, reporting that one young man was spotted behind a screen at one with his hand on his girlfriend's breast.6

Chicago's sinners, however, still managed to get much greater attention than her reformers, although both could be loud and vigorous and earthy in their efforts. Alson J. Smith described what was different about the city's vice besides the number of "separate acts:"

> It was this open, unblushing bawdiness, so different from the back-alley whoring of the East, that captured the imagination of a whole series of writers including Edna Ferber (who got a lot of North Clark Street into "Show-Boat"), Dreiser and Ben Hecht...7

"Successful vice," according to Alson Smith, "was as much a part of the Chicago story as successful meat-packing or successful railroading or successful farm machinery manufacturing."8

The city's open vice area was the Levee, from Polk Street south to 22nd Street along Dearborn and Clark Streets. Alson Smith said such districts, "for better or for worse, were of the essence of the city." He called them, "part and parcel of a brash, brawling, bawdy city that was chronologically and geographically close to the frontier and glad of it. They were an integral part of Chicago's self-conscious bigness; no other city in the world could boast of so much vice, such elaborate bagnios, such colorful madames, such a phalanx of demi-mondes." Smith adds:

"In giving flavor to Chicago, the Armours, Swifts and Ryersons must take a back seat to (Hinky Dink) Kenna, (Big Jim) Colosimo, Capone and the Everleigh sisters."

The Everleigh sisters, Minna and Ada, were the most famous representatives of the Levee in the first dozen years of this century. The two First Ward aldermen, Bathhouse John Coughlin and Hinky Dink Kenna, however, gave them both competition for the title. The Everleigh sisters held the slightly more honorable jobs of being madames.

The Everleigh Club represented a much higher degree of sophistication than did, for example, Black May's, which was infamous for bestiality as well as sex, or the House of All Nations with its $2 and $5 entrances. The Everleighs charged a basic $50 and had a $15,000 piano and $650 gold-plated spittoons in the elaborately decorated rooms of their mansion-brothel on South Dearborn Street.

Minna Everleigh in words of advice she gave to women starting to work in her establishment showed better than the $650 spittoons what the city's world-famous brothel represented:

> Be polite and forget what you are here for. Gentlemen are only gentlemen when properly introduced. We shall see that each girl is properly presented to each guest. No lining up for selection as in other houses.
>
> It's going to be difficult at first, I know. It means, briefly, that your language will have to be lady-like and that you will forget the entreaties you have used in the past. You have the whole night before you, and one $50 client is more desirable than five $10 ones. Less wear and tear. You will thank me for the advice in later years. Your youth and beauty are all you have. Preserve it. Stay respectable by all means.
>
> We know men better than you do. Don't rush'em or roll'em. We will permit no monkeyshines, no knockout drops, no robberies, no crimes of any description. We supply the clients. You amuse them in a way they've never been amused before. Give, but give interestingly and with mystery.[9]

Near the end of Chicago's world's fair generation, the reformers finally succeeded in closing the Levee down. The first to go, by fiat of

Mayor Carter Harrison II, was the Everleigh Club. Foreseeing the tightening down of Chicago's vice district, proprietor Ike Bloom proposed to the Everleigh sisters an elaborate plan to get the prostitutes to go to church and to bribe some of the zealous clergyman. Even the Everleigh sisters, however, knew the end had come and quietly dropped out of the business.

Chicago, in the 1920s, would again open up and become the speakeasy town famous for its gangsters and free-flowing booze, but that reputation would lack the vital and open sensuality that had marked the Levee. Never again would tourists discover the Everleigh Club or the famous, bawdy annual First Ward Ball sponsored at the turn-of-the-century by Hinky Dink Kenna and Bathhouse John Coughlin and patronized religiously by the denizens of the Levee.10

The era of the 192Os in the United States, however, with its changed sexual mores,and experimentation was in many ways fathered in Chicago at the turn-of-the-century The "Bohemian" life of the city was dormant for all but a handful of writers for half a generation between the closing of Chicago's Levee in 1913 and the opening of the roaring 1920s throughout the country. Through their writings, Edna Ferber, Theodore Dreiser, Ben Hecht, Sherwood Anderson and Floyd Dell helped hand it on as a butterfly to the flapper generation.

The Town Everyone Wanted to Reform

1. Julian Ralph, a New Yorker, writing in 1893 described Chicago's robust sensuallty as "Russian":

> They eat and drink like Russians, and, from their fondness for surrounding themselves with bright and elegant women, I gather that they love like Russians. In like manner, do they spend their money. In New York heavy drinking in the clubs is going out of fashion, and there is less and less high play at cards; but in Chicago, as in St. Petersburg, the wine flows freely, the stakes are high.

2. Julian Ralph, "Our Great West" (Harper & Bros., 1893)

3. Dr. James Conway collects the morally righteous volumes that proliferated in the city during this era. Among tbe titles about the Windy City in this era were: "Chicago and Its Cess-pools of Infamy" by Samuel Paynter Wilson, "Fighting the Debauchery of Our Boys and Girls" by Rev. Phillip Yarrow and "Wicked City" published in and about Chicago in 1906 by Grant Eugene Stevens. The latter—Chicago-style—had a rather curious promotion attached to it. Readers by finding hidden clues in the book could win a 2-karat diamond ring, a summer cottage, a piano or other prizes. The book sold for $2.50 and included an ode to Chicago by the author (dedicated to the members of the Commercial Club) which contained verses such as:

> From scandal perches they did bawl,
> wickedest city in the world;
> Branding it deep upon our city wall
> The fading name "windy" smothered by the
> new one hurled.

4. The gentility of Chicago had a name for Mayor Harrison that said much. He was called simply, "Our Carter."

5. Stephen Longstreet in 1973 wrote a book titled "Chicago" about this era's sensuality and subtitled his work: "An Intimate Portrait of People, Pleasures and Power: 1860-1919." A disappointment! It cleans up the grammar in this very famous Chicago quotation, attributed the quote to "George Wellington Wheeler and calls the man who tried to claim a hunk of the lake simply a "Chicago landseller." What's particularly inappropriate about it all is that the author unfortunately used the quote to begin Chapter I, shaking a reader's confidence. The book tells interesting stories about the period without capturing any of its themes. A wonderful, warm, sensual book about Chicago

during the period could be enthralling. Lloyd Wendt and Herman Kogan come much closer in "Lords of the Levee" (Bobbs-Merrill Co., 1943), later published as "Bosses in Lusty Old Chicago." A fascinating history of vice and crime in Chicago is "Gem of the Prairie" (Alfred A. Knopf, 1940) by Herbert Asbury, which is packed with colorful details of the city's sins and sensuality.

6. Bessie Louise Pierce, "As Others See Chicago" (University of Chicago, 1933) p.489.

7. "The Social Evil in Chicago" (The Vice Commission of the City of Chicago, 1911) p.250 made some stinging arguments against wide-open vice that are worth considering today.

8. The report stated: "The first truth that the Commission desires to impress upon its citizens of Chicago is that prostitution is a commercialized business with tremendous profits...controlled largely by men, not women. Separate the male exploiters from the problem and we minimize its extent."

9. The commission zeroed in on the fact that the police were given power to establish arbitrary rules and uncertain regulations, thus making them the enactors and enforcers of the law, which is always bad news for society.

10. The report also hit the double standard of morality that ran through the whole issue. Without specifically mentioning the Everleigh Club, the report states that clubs patronized by the rich were never raided while the poorer clubs frequently were.

11. The rampant discrimination against blacks was also denounced in the commission's document. Black neighborhoods were taken over as vice areas and blacks were hired to perform the menial jobs in the clubs. Children who lived in the vice districts were exposed to everything that went on there, and were used to sell candy, gum and other items.

12. There was a never-ending need for more women. The report didn't use the phrase "white slave traffic," but only because that phrase implies that all the victims were white. Many were not. The business fed upon tragedy, loneliness, and poverty to get a fresh supply of prostitutes.

13. Finally, it was the woman who suffered, not the man. He escaped as a "romantizer." "It is not just," the report concluded.

14. Alson Smith, "Chicago's Left Bank" (Henry Regnery Co., 1953) p.136.

15. Alson Smith's "Syndicate City" (Regnery, 1954) updates "Gem of the Prairie" and Ovid Demaris's "Captive City" (Lyle Stuart, 1969) continued where Smith left off.

16. Charles Washburn, "Come Into My Parlor" (National Library Press, 1934) p.24. Washburn, did a delightful and well-crafted biography of the sisters with their cooperation. They seemed to have believed deeply that their class and style justified them in contrast to other brothels. Wealth, not style, in the end was tbe basis of the Everleigh Club's respect and acceptance.

17. Equally important to the continuity of Chicago's vice history has been the corruption of its police force. In approximately 1908,.it was Chicago Chief of Police George Shippy who demonstrated the caliber of Chicago gendarmes by saying, "I stay home at night with my family. That's why I don't see what's going on."

Eugene Field, Chicago's Puckish John the Baptist

The John the Baptist of the Chicagoization of America was Eugene Field, a puckish journalist best known today as the author of the poems "Little Boy Blue" and "Wynken, Blynken and Nod."

From 1883 until his untimely death in 1895, his column "Sharps and Flats" in Victor Lawson's the *Morning News* paper (later, the *Chicago Record*) prepared the way for the city's greatness.

Eugene Field would warn time and again in his pixieish way of the excesses of the fatuous culture of the East.

He was to show the way from so many different vantage points, to do so much and to affect so many, but he was not the one who was to come. He was not the evolution For, despite all he did and said, he did not bring the gospel of Chicago: the conviction, insight and serendipitous discovery that even urban America could be democratized.

Field would have bellowed out loud at such a comparison,would have written a satirical poem about it and then would have drawn a preposterous sketch of himself in the desert. But the comparison, nevertheless, is apt.

Field found the language that was to be used. His biographer, Slason Thompson, estimated that he wrote over 7,000,000 words in his columns published day in and day out.[1] And they were read, intensely read, in the newspaper that as a result of him acquired the largest circulation in the city.

The feature he wrote had as many as 40 items a day in it, much of it poetry. He was a wordsmith who chipped off his language whether it was prose or poetry and a teacher who helped others to do it.

Those whose prose has flair and individuality have very often learned their wordcraft by first writing poetry.[2] And, in Field's day, verse in the United States was possibly more important and more revered than ever before or after. America was in the process of learning not only to speak but also to write a language of her own.

The schools were sharply aware of the function of poetry and paid daily attention to the memorization and reciting of poetry.[2] And Eugene Field filled the school's insatiable demand for such in a language simple enough not only for children but also for America.

"Little Boy Blue" was far and away the most popular of all such verse. But there were others: "To my Old Coat." "The Sugar Plum Tree," "The Oak and the Ivy," altogether several volumes.

Schools for decades after his death held regular Eugene Field programs dedicated to the recital of his poetry. The State of Missouri proclaimed an annual Eugene Field Day for its schools. Special Eugene Field dictionaries were on hand to help the youngsters with the few difficult words in his poems.

For a nation scratching to learn a new, a simpler, a common language, much can be said for such rote learning. Field himself was among the first to damn it as an education, however. He wasn't, as in so many areas, able to offer alternatives. They would come from the Chicago he was preparing, from Francis Parker,Ella Flagg Young and from John Dewey.

In his pre-Chicago days as a managing editor of the Denver Tribune,[3] Field seemed on the verge of encouraging a wholesale rebellion of children against the country's very regimented school system He openly encouraged them, tongue-in-cheek in the kind of deviltry he was famous for throughout his life. This included newspaper exhortations about the sheer joy of playing in mud, smearing "the Yellow Custard" of a caterpillar on school walls or putting a bent nail on the teacher's seat.[4]

What stifled this invitation to rebellion by Field is unknown, although it might have been that his own children were reaching the age where such antics were becoming options. The oldest was eight when they moved to Chicago. His children were high-spirited and "wild," which a friend attributed to the fact that "their father used to frolic with them much of the time and allowed them the freedom that made them so intense in their play."

It was not only children whom Field worked at teaching the common language. His column was open to the poetry of others and it encouraged people to write verse by its very presence. Specifically, he stimulated such Chicago writers as Theodore Dreiser, George Ade and

Edgar Lee Masters. He helped show them poetry and journalism as stepping stones to other, often more permanent, forms of literature.

Eugene Field did something else for these writers and for Chicago. He turned them away from the East as the model for culture. His biographer Thompson wrote:

> It is more than probable that Eugene Field chose Chicago for the place of his permanent abode after deliberately weighing the advantages and limitations of its situation with reference to his literary career. He felt that it was as far east as he could make his home without coming within the influence of those social and literary conventions that have squeezed so much of genuine American flavor out of our literature. He had received many tempting offers from New York newspapers before coming to Chicago, and after our acquaintance I do not believe a year went by that Field did not decline an engagement, personally tendered by Mr. Dana, to go to the *New York Sun*, at a salary nearly double that he was receiving here. But, as he told Julian Ralph on one occasion, he would not live in, or write for, the East. For, as he put it, there was more liberty and fewer literary "fellers" out West, and a man had more chance to be judged on his merits and "grow up with the country."[5]

And when Easterners, prestigious and erudite, presumed to visit Chicago during Eugene Field's writing days, he twitted them unmercifully. He named names and bedeviled the rich, culturally-conscious Chicagoan who had extended the invitation. Specifically, he detailed how the native had made his fortune, especially if he did so through the slaughter yards or allied industries. And he indulged in mock obsequience, to the Bostonian or New Yorker as in the following poem about Edmund C. Steadman:

> We're cleaning up the boulevards
>
> And divers thoroughfares;
>
> Our lawn, our fences, and our yards
>
> Are bristling with repairs;

And soon Chicago'll be abloom
With splendor and renown;
For ain't we going to have a boom
When Steadman comes to town?[6]

Field also wrote a "Sharps and Flats" column about the events in which he described whimsically a long, grand parade that would greet Steadman and include among other elements:

A brass band, afoot
Another brass band
A beautiful young woman playing the guitar
symbolizing Apollo and his lute
in a car drawn by
nine milk white stallions impersonating the muses.
Two hundred Chicago poets afoot.

He was not mightily impressed with Chicagoans who imitated New York culture and wrote that "the crème de la crème of our elite lift up their hands, and groan, when they discover that it takes as long to play a classic symphony as it does to slaughter a carload of Missouri razor-backs, or an invoice of prairie racers from Kansas."

Many of his biting comments reflect the city's self-consciousness that it was Porkopolis or rather dismay that the packers were not self-conscious. He evinces no awareness, however, of the working conditions in the stockyards that socially-conscious writers would later expose.

In some ways, Field was at best struggling to be more socially conscious the last few years of his life. In 1887 he had not a drop of sympathy for the men hanged as a result of "Haymarket Riot hysteria" and wrote a nationally famous poem praising a civil war veteran who interrupted their funeral procession to march at the head of it with an American flag in protest.

In 1894, the combination of his friendship with labor leader Eugene Debs and the derision of George Pullman, (whom he branded as "The Markeesy di Pullman") still left him untouched by the cause of the Pullman strikers. Knowing the two men, and admitting that a person had a hundred times better chance to get succor and sympathy from Debs than Pullman, Field still couldn't understand the social issues in the strike of 1894 and said that his friend Debs was to be spoken of "rather in pity than anger."

Field was neither a democrat nor a Democrat, but a staunch Republican.[7] He wrote militantly in behalf of that party's candidates, although there is no evidence he ever got around to voting for anyone.

In his last three years, he became rather esoteric in his devotion to the verse of the Roman poet Horace, and his love of books and manuscripts.[8] He also, however, wrote warmly of the foibles and problems of a family attempting to own at last their own home in the suburbs. The difference between the problems of that family and the survival ones of the people described in "The Jungle" by Upton Sinclair (10 years later) lay bare much that happened between when Eugene Field hoed the ground and when others such as Sinclair reaped.

For many the confrontation of 1894 with Pullman was the turning point of Chicago's conscience. The city sympathized with Debs and the strikers. The bitter strike made Eugene Field more serious and more sober, according to Robert Conrow in his book, "Field Days." He was perhaps too set in his ways, however to be as turned around as others were.

And, one of the ways in which Field was set was that he was, in person, a very unserious and unsober individual. He was a practical joker of the wildest proportions and often put preposterous material in his column just so the editor would have something to strike out.

This side of Field appeared in his "sub rosa" writing, much of which didn't appear in print until long after his death. He wrote, for example, a poem every bit as charming as "Little Boy Blue" titled "Little Willie":[9]

When Willie was a little boy,
    No more than five or six,
Right constantly he did annoy
    His mother with his tricks.
Yet, not a picayune cared I
    For what he did or said,
Unless, as happened frequently,
    The rascal wet the bed.

Closely he cuddled up to me,
    And put his hands in mine,
Till all at once I seemed to be

Afloat in seas of brine.
Sabean odors clogged the air,
And filled my soul with dread,
Yet I could only grin and bear
When Willie wet the bed.

After two more nose titillating verses, Eugene Field explains that it was all long ago and now Willie has little Willies of his own who do what he used to do. He ends with a stanza that was too ribald to surface with the first four, when they were finally published. The last stanza read:

Had I my choice, no shapely dame
Should share my couch with me
No amorous jade of tarnished fame,
Nor wench of high degree;
But I would choose and choose again
The little curly head,
Who cuddled close beside me when
He used to wet the bed.[10]

The schools that idolized Eugene Field would have been even more astounded by other of Field's nonpublished Rabelaisan poems and, in one instance, a short story.

His wild sense of humor and his penchant for the sensual were joined when his wife suggested they acquire a "doctor's book or two" to save on household bills and to cure "our little household ills." Field responded with his usual sense of imagination by suggesting they acquire the works of Dr. Rabelais, not informing his spouse that the works were "venal" rather than medical. But, a month or two later, when a child was "croupy," his wife consulted the volumes of Dr. Rabelais and Field was exposed. The works were later to prove a help to him when his ever present dyspepsia grew worse. And his wife was glad to have them for him:

And still at night, when all the rest
Are hushed in sweet repose,
O'er those two interdicted tomes
I laugh and nod and doze.

From worldly ills and business cares
My weary mind is lured,
And by that doctor's magic art
My ailments all are cured.

So my dear, knowing little wife
Is glad that it is so,
And with a smile recalls the trick
I played her years ago;
And whensoe'er dyspeptic pangs
Compel me to their sway,
The saucy girl bids me consult
My Doctor Rabelais.

There were other poems in which his jolly pen wrote of priapisms, thrusting spears and the "frail spot that lies beneath your girdle." His ribaldness was one more barrier that he knocked down without going beyond it. In his age, such sensual matters were not often written about in America (except in tirades by the reformers). Field smashed that taboo, but he did it only for his male acquaintances, not for society and above all, not for an open society of both men and women.

Still, there is no question that his taste in the erotic was passed on and eventually incorporated into Chicago's sensual vitality.

At the age of 45, on Nov. 2, 1895, Eugene Field died in the night as the result of a heart attack. He quickly achieved nationwide immortality. People were to twist and distort him to a saccharin sweetness even through he had tried to head this off with an "Auto-analysis" that said not a word about Chicago as such but told a lot about its John the Baptist. After several pages of chronological biography, he concluded:11

I dislike "politics," so called.

I should like to have the privilege of voting ex tended to women

I am unalterably opposed to capital punishment.

I favor a system of pensions for noble services in literature, art, science, etc.

I approve of compulsory education.

If I had my way, I should make the abuse of horses, dogs, and cattle a penal offense; I should abolish all dog laws and dog-catchers, and I would punish severely everybody who caught and caged birds.

I dislike all exercise and play all games very indifferently.

I love to read in bed.

I believe in churches and schools: I hate wars, armies, soldiers, guns, and fireworks.

I like music (limited).

I have been a great theater goer.

I enjoy the society of doctors and clergymen.

My favorite color is red.

I do not care particularly for sculpture or for paintings; I try not to become interested in them, for the reason that if I were to cultivate a taste for them I should presently become hopelessly bankrupt.

I am extravagantly fond of perfumes.

I am a poor diner, and I drink no wine or spirits of any kind; I do not smoke tobacco.

I dislike crowds and I abominate functions.

I am six feet in height; am of spare build, weigh 160 pounds, and have shocking taste in dress.

But I like to have well-dressed people about me.

My eyes are blue, my complexion pale, my face is shaven, and I incline to baldness.

It is only when I look and see how young and fair and sweet my wife is that I have a good opinion of myself.

I am fond of the companionship of women, and I have no unconquerable prejudices against feminine beauty. I recall with pride that in twenty-two years of active journalism I have always written in reverential praise of womankind.

I favor early marriage.

I do not love all children.

I have tried to analyze my feelings toward children, and I think I discover that I love them in so far as I can make pets of them.

I believe that, if I live, I shall do my literary work when I am a grandfather.

Eugene Field

1. Slason Thompson's two-volume life "Eugene Field: A Study in Heredity and Contradictions" (Charles Scribner's Sons, 1901) is a very thorough biography of Field that tends to overkill with pedantic, factual information about him, such as the scores of bowling matches between Field and the author. On the other hand, the work contains many of the bits and pieces including sketches (nonsensical) and personal letters that were as much him as was his writing for publication.

2. Here is a small stock of wordsmith Field's expressions: "paragraphists of the press"; "japes, bourds and mockages aside"; "poor as Job's historic turkey"; "the slangy pen of the daily newspaper writer"; "growly-powly as a bear"; and "from out of the wormhole of forgotten years." He, for a number of years, used a group of trite expressions such as: "We opine," "Anent the story," and "It is stated, though not authoritatively." He quit these "country journalisms," however, when his friends put a mock column of them in the paper when he was off on a trip.

3. Field was born in Missouri, specifically in St. Louis in the year 1850. His father was a scholarly lawyer, who defended the slave, Dred Scott, in the most famous trial of the era.

4. The dark humor of Field's "Tribune Primer" (Denver, 1882) becomes lighter the more one reads, not only the individual, one-paragraph essays but also the pattern of his preposterousness. An original copy of it sells for more than $5,000 today.

5. Slason Thompson, "Eugene Field" (Charles Scribner's Sons, 1901) Vol. I, p.193. Eugene Field, on the other hand, could be quite sardonic about his chosen city. He compared its literary growth with the increase in the packinghouse trade and wrote: "The packer has patronized the poet; metaphorically speaking, the hog and the epic have lain down together and wallowed in the same Parnassian pool. The censers that have swung continually in the temples of the muses have been replenished with lard oil, and to our grateful olfactories has the joyous Lake breezes wafted the refreshing odors of sonnets and of slaughter pens commingled."

6. Ibid., Vol. I, p.341. Field's Republican politics hail back to his youth and the party of Abraham Lincoln. He never forgave the Democratic party its "copperheadism" during the Civil War. He was even more critical of independents, especially any who had in any way supported Grover Cleveland, a Democratic president from New York.

7. One of the reasons that Field failed to become part of the Chicago revolution that he had helped instigate was that he became very deeply involved with books rather than people during his last six years. Slason Thompson divided his 12 years in Chicago into two 6-year periods: the first

taken up with people "of his own kind" and the second, with books. Published posthumously was his volume, "The Love Affairs of a Bibliomaniac" Privately printed, 1896).

8. The cover-up of Eugene Field's Rabelaisan nature by his biographers Slason Thompson, Francis Wilson and Charles Dennis is elaborated on by Robert Conrow in "Field Days" (Charles Scribner's Sons, 1974) p.118. Francis Wilson claimed rather preposterously that he had never heard his friend Field "tell a squeamish story." Thompson in a 1927 revision of his authoritative biography finally acknowledged the existence of the poem "Little Willie" but omitted the final verse. Charles Dennis put Field "in corsets with an incipient halo." Conrow doesn't say it, but these biographers were writing for a market (such as the libraries of schools named after him) that would have shuddered at Little Willie wetting the bed.

9. Conrow, p.116.

10. His "Auto-analysis" was written in the winter of 1894. It was, according to Field's introduction to it, "for the information of those who, for one reason or another, are applying constantly to me for biographical data concerning myself." Thompson argued that in it Field was "laughing up his sleeve at us...so cleverly are truth and fiction dove-tailed together" in the piece. He said that Field constantly distorts or changes little facts such as the order in which his books were published as "a notification to his intimates that the whole thing was not to be taken as a serious bibliology of his works or index of his character." Actually, just the opposite probably should be implied. Field stated much that was true and gave some indications of deep, almost teasing self-perception; but he had to put off his intimate associates in doing so as his practical jokes were to keep them, not the world, off balance. Consequently, his distortion was in the little things.

11. Thompson, Vol. I, p.235.

Part II

The Word and the Line are Changed

People who want to protect culture from change attempt to make it complicated. They who are able to simplify, however, create change. In 1893 Chicago, "they" meant the people. Chicagoans chose simple new words and lines, thus unleashing their language, art and architecture to storm American culture. And there was, therefore, change.

Newspapers Start Selling for a Penny

Chicago was the scene of many journalistic revolutions, but perhaps the most important one occurred in November, 1895, when the morning papers started selling for a penny each.

A few penny newspapers had existed before that date and the most famous of them all was in Chicago. It was Victor Lawson's *Chicago Daily News*, which had been selling for one cent for almost 20 years, since its inception in 1876. In 1895, it had the largest circulation in the city, 210,000.

Still, the actual evolution was not in full throb until the aloof and dignified *Chicago Tribune* proclaimed that it would start selling for a penny.1 The shot reverberated first in the offices of the city's other morning newspapers and then in all the other major cities in the country. Even Lawson, according to his editor, Charles Dennis, had sought the "better" readers (the ones who would respond to ads). Now, the *Tribune* was finding the way to the doors of the "back alley" people of the city who had little more than their pennies to offer.

That decision changed newspapers drastically because it altered their readership.2 Within months, for example, the *Chicago Tribune* made innovations that were to become new directions in journalism. And they were begun because the price of the paper changed.

The *Chicago Daily News* had begun the journalistic revolution in 1876, when it was started as a penny newspaper by Melville Stone and William Dougherty. Lawson bought it out within months and the circulation skyrocketed so that it had the highest circulation in the city within a decade. Other newspapers, however, didn't follow Lawson's lead, even though he showed that such a paper could get advertising and be a financial success.3 He didn't even follow it himself when he started a morning newspaper known at first as the *Morning News* and subsequently as the *News-Record* and finally the *Record*. The paper was begun in 1881, but continued to sell for 2 cents until 1888.

Economics was not the only reason the revolution did not take place. Circulation was simply not the all-important goal of newspapers. That would have been too democratic for the many Chicago journals that represented rather the viewpoints of the millionaires who bought and sold them and, even more important, the advertisers who were the main source of revenue. Circulation was something you lied about.

The *Chicago Times* (not related to the present *Chicago Sun-Times*) proclaimed in a box on the top right-hand side of the front page during the 1890s: "The *Times* is an Advertising Medium Reaching the Best People of Chicago and the Northwest."

That was the thinking that was meant to sell advertisers, who were supposedly interested only in reaching those with enough money to buy their products.

There were no checks of actual circulation.4 The corrupt traction magnate Charles T. Yerkes bought the once prestigious *Inter-Ocean* to rail against the other papers, which were railing against his success at bribing 80 to 90 percent of the City Council to get streetcar ordinances passed. Little matter the paper had only a 4,000 circulation, he could claim any figure he wanted.

The *Chicago Times* also served principally a political purpose well into the 1890s. It too had one of the most interesting histories among Chicago newspapers. The *Times* had been owned at one time by Sen. Stephen A. Douglas, the man who ran against Abraham Lincoln for United States senator and later for President. During the Civil War, it was temporarily closed down by the military for its Copperhead or pro-Southern views. President Lincoln personally lifted the ban. Wilbur Storey, the *Times'* editor and publisher, became internationally famous for his individualistic style of journalism and especially for headlines such as the one about a southern hanging which read:

> Jerked to Jesus—Two of Them, in Louisiana, Died with the Sweet Confidence of Pious People, While Yet Two Others, In Mississippi, Expired Exhorting the Public To Beware of Sisters-In-Law.

All in all, "Old Storey" was a lively and exciting editor, before becoming mentally unbalanced near the end of his life in 1884.

In the 1890s, Carter Harrison the Elder bought the withering *Times* as a political organ to promote his candidacy for reelection as mayor of Chicago in 1893. He won, and his sons continued the paper for a short time after he was assassinated. Again, circulation wasn't as important as the prestige. Neither did much good for the Harrison family member's finances as the paper lost half their fortune.

Victor Lawson helped to turn the circulation issue around by publishing daily the numbers of papers sold, putting his signature on the figures and swearing they were accurate. He also was proclaiming by the late 1880s that the *Chicago Daily News* had a total circulation higher than that of the rest of the papers combined.5

The *Chicago Tribune* was one other paper that prospered despite the tremendous circulation advantage held by Victor Lawson's *Daily News* and the *Morning News*. The *Tribune*, founded in 1847, made up in advertising and prestige what it lacked in circulation, or so it felt.

The *Tribune* was very much the vehicle for the personal and often creative journalism of Joseph Medill. He had helped found the Republican Party while he and the paper were credited with propelling Lincoln into the White House. He lost out in the struggle for control of the *Tribune* near the end of the Civil War, although he retained a connection with the paper. In 1871, he was elected, in the aftermath of the city's major fire, mayor of Chicago. He resigned and did not complete his full two-year term. In 1874, he bought controlling interest in the paper and served as its editor and publisher until his death in 1899.

Medill was a Republican and the paper was an avowed partisan journal. It had moved away from many of his views from 1865 to 1873, when he was not editor, but his return brought it back to the Republican party of Ulysses S. Grant, although arguing for free trade and against the Republican idea of high tariffs.

Medill had international views that were just a little short of imperialistic and some concepts of Americanism that had little tolerance for any radicals. When the issue was journalism, his standard was excellence and quality. The paper often scooped the nation and carried the by-lines of the best writers in the world. No matter what the circulation story, the *Tribune* remained the best-known Chicago paper nationally and internationally.

The change in direction of journalism that resulted from the price reduction can be seen in the following passage from Vol. 3 of the "The Chicago Tribune: Its First Hundred Years," published by the company and written by Philip Kinsley:

> The Chicago newspaper world was swept by a circulation storm of hurricane proportions in the latter part of 1895. The *Tribune* led the way by reducing its price to one cent, taking in 25,000 new subscriptions the first day after this announcement.[6] This was a radical departure for the *Tribune* circulation department, which was founded on the theory that "quality" circulation only was wanted. People living in back alleys with no money to spend in the stores had not been sought. Now the day of mass circulation was started.[7]

The 1893 to 1895 Depression and the fact that Victor Lawson's morning paper was doing well with names such as George Ade, Eugene Field and John McCutcheon were unmentioned factors. Still, all the reasons in the world could have piled up at the newspaper's door without the editors opening it. The editors did yank it, and thereby initiated a number of major changes in journalism, or perhaps it was the "back alley" people who did.

On November 10 came the actual reduction to one cent for a daily and 5 cents for a Sunday paper and, with it, the following editorial:

> The *Tribune* in doing this is the first of the great newspapers of the world to place all the resources of a first-class modern journal within the reach of all the people and to recognize the equality of all readers by putting its price on the broadest democratic base.

It should be noted that even the use of that word "democratic" was a significant change for a paper such as the *Tribune*. That word, even with a small "d" was the language of the other party. The editorial continued:

> Thanks to the people the *Tribune* has had nearly half a century of uninterrupted prosperity. It believes that the path to more prosperity is to share with the people the reduction in the cost of the paper, printing, telegraph dispatches and some other items in the production of a newspaper. The *Tribune* has been a pioneer in the popularization of price. It has twice before made a reduction. It was the price only which was cheapened, not the newspaper. This will be our policy now. More pains and more money than ever before will be spent in the effort to make the *Tribune* the best newspaper in the world. Success succeeds, and in sharing its success with its readers the *Tribune* has faith that once more the people's gain will be its gain. For 40 years the *Tribune* has held its place as the first newspaper of Chicago and the accepted spokesman for the health and wealth, culture and conscience of this great city, and the country of which Chicago is the emporium. The *Tribune*'s best prospectus is in its past. It has always sought to serve the people, and at more than one critical moment has defended their interests at the risk of great sacrifices to itself. Its highest ambition is to be recognized as the Tribune of the People.

Among those who might have gulped at that description of the *Tribune*'s past were labor leader Eugene Debs, who at the time was in jail serving a questionable six month contempt of court sentence to the satisfaction of the *Tribune*. Illinois Governor John Peter Altgeld might have objected. He had just stung the paper by pardoning one of its employees who had embezzled from the *Tribune*. Altgeld's argument in doing it was that the man had seen his employers get by with questionable behavior and had partially been led astray by their bad example.

Another Chicagoan who certainly read the words carefully was Victor Lawson. His newspapers were summarily dismissed in the editorial when the *Tribune* claimed it was "the first of the great newspapers in the world" to sell at such a low price. Lawson's papers were among the more prominent in the world and were credited with many innovations, not the least of which was the first regular columnist in

Eugene Field. In addition, George Ade and John McCutcheon were among his writers (McCutcheon eventually became more famous as a *Tribune* cartoonist). Lawson, however, according to his managing editor Charles Dennis, didn't actually set advertising rates by the number of copies sold but by "how many went into homes where people could afford to buy advertising," Hugh Duncan reports in "The Rise of Chicago as a Literary Center."

The *Tribune*, nevertheless, had always stayed close to the people almost in spite of itself, simply because Joseph Medill so deeply believed in Chicago and the city's ways. He gave no quarter to the East nor to any culture or snobbery it wanted to import to his Chicago. He was often an imaginative, positive thinker whose editorials were controversial and thoroughly Republican. They were strongly researched and well-written, a tradition with the paper ever since.

And even though the *Tribune* was critical of Lincoln at times during the Civil War, attempting to promote and demote generals left and right, it retained a bond with the great Illinois man of the people. Medill and Lincoln were on warm personal terms and the *Tribune* editor passed on Lincoln stories and philosophy until just before the editor's death. That bond was an important one in Chicago's history.

At first, the changes in the *Tribune* after it took in the "back alley" people were scarcely noticeable. The *Tribune* continued to fight Yerkes's efforts to steal the city's streetcar rights-of-way and seemed to fight harder than ever. It also gave out free Chicago streetcar tickets with subscriptions.

In advertising, it emphasized one-cent sales in the various department stores. Lawson, years before, was credited with starting the popular 99 cent or $1.99 prices on items so people would have the penny left over to buy his paper in an era when pennies were in short supply. The *Tribune* now promoted heavily in stores, "Tribune One-Cent Bargain Sales" to emphasize its new price. The stores got considerable free publicity as pictures of shoppers loaded down with all they had bought for a total of 11 or 15 cents were featured.

And what of the news? The *Tribune* in 1895 promoted possibly the sharpest newspaper man in the country to be city editor. He was James Keeley, 28 years old. In subsequent years, he would become managing editor and in 1910, assume control of the paper. He ran the paper until 1914, when he left to become editor of the *Chicago Herald* and to make room for the *Tribune* to be run by its two young owners, first cousins

Joseph Patterson and Robert McCormick.

As city editor of the *Chicago Tribune* in 1895, Keeley formulated his concept that "News is a commodity and for sale like any other commodity."[8] That definition showed the hard-core practicality of the city editor who once stumbled on a late-night meeting of the high financiers of Chicago and told them, "since you sent for me, what do you want of me?" No one realized that none of them had, and Keeley got an exclusive on a major bank going under. More important, the commodity concept of news took the emphasis away from the publisher and the advertisers and placed it with the penny customers.

A glance at the paper during that era gives a reader a sense of what news is. The thought is often expressed today that the competition of TV and radio has taken the urgency and immediacy out of the newspapers that they had in the days of the extras and of newsboys proclaiming the breaking stories. However, newspapers still enjoy the discipline of having to sell the news rather than give it away as radio and television do. And Keeley found the penny readers the most alive audience newspapers ever had in this country. They bought up to half a dozen papers a day and they compared. These are the best readers a writer can have.

Tribune editor Keeley would make himself and his paper best for "personal service." As Keeley stated it:

> The big development of the modern newspaper will be along the lines of personal service. The newspaper that not only informs and instructs its readers but is of service is the one that commands attention, gets circulation, and also holds its readers after it gets them. The newspaper must be of service today, not only in politics and morals...but it must be of social service. It must not only plead with the people to swat the crook, but it must urge them to swat the fly.
>
> The newspaper must not only help in fighting for a clean city, but must aid the clergy in the fight for a clean home. It must not only teach patriotism but must show the folly of the annual massacre on July 4 (from fireworks)—a slaughter doubly horrible because it is done in the name of patriotism. It must enter into the everyday life of its readers and, like the parish priest,

> be guide, counselor and friend...I don't mind telling you confidentially that the results of my efforts to put this into practice have been extremely satisfactory financially...9

The "democratization" of the *Tribune,* geared as it was even to people who "scarcely read," brought a new push for means to print photos in the paper. The daily paper had usually carried only one or two engravings or etchings on key pages. The Sunday papers—especially the *Tribune*—were profuse with them and were typographically beautiful papers. The *Tribune* at this time experimented with the copper halftones from photographs. They weren't perfected but they gave the paper possibly the first full picture page of any paper in history.

The *Tribune,* as well as the *Chronicle* and *Inter-Ocean,* which joined the *Tribune* at one cent, became more aware of the needs of poorer Chicagoans. They sponsored various fund raising projects to help the needy, including a Christmas fund to give dolls to the poor at Christmas.

Joseph Medill is often misquoted with a heartless comment from the early 1880s to the effect that the poor and unemployed ought to be given a painless poison. The facetious comment appeared in the paper under a 1870 suburban reporter's by-line. Medill has since been maligned by its attribution to him. Now, however, his newspaper began a crusade that has never received the same attention as it campaigned with the slogan "No man, woman or child shall be hungry tonight." It urged the chief of police and mayor "to feed them first and inquire later."10

Other changes in the *Tribune* were not as socially meaningful, but had long range impact.

It was just a little thing, but it said something. The paper had always been militantly against boxing. From its earliest years, it had looked down on the rough plebeian form of brutality. Suddenly, the *Tribune* was found giving the fight between James J. Corbett and Bob Fitzsimmons daily build up publicity and then via wire a blow by blow description filling four columns.

The *Tribune,* in its democratization even came out in favor of the shocking new fad of bloomers. Although it did add a few reservations, it said men shouldn't dictate women's fashions.

Newspapers Start Selling for a Penny

Of much longer duration in its effects on journalist history was the change in the *Tribune*'s approach to covering sports. With its new readership, the definition of sports broadened as did the paper's coverage. It now became, especially on Sunday, a separate section of the paper set off by its pink color.

Equally important was the change in the comics. The *Tribune* increased the new journalistic innovation to four pages.

It was another innovation, something that other papers had done and which the *Tribune* had looked upon somewhat disdainfully.

The real democratization of the *Tribune* was simply that it had an effect by getting into the hand of people who might not have been able to buy a paper as easily in the morning. Much can be made of the editorial differences in Chicago newspapers at various times in their histories, but their strength often lies in a common bond Jane Addams once spoke of:

> The newspapers, in a frank reflection of popular demand, exhibit an omnivorous curiosity equally insistent upon the trivial and the important. They are perhaps the most obvious manifestations of that desire to know, that "What is this?" and "Why do you do that?" of the child. The first dawn of social consciousness takes this form, as the dawning intelligence of the child takes the form of constant question and insatiate curiosity...
>
> Partly through this wide reading of human life, we find in ourselves a new affinity for all men, which probably never existed in the world before. Evil itself does not shock us as it once did, and we count only that man merciful in whom we recognize an understanding of the criminal. We have learned as common knowledge that much of the insensitivity and hardness of the world is due to the lack of imagination which prevents a realization of the experiences of other people.11

The one penny experiment of the Chicago newspapers lasted only three years as emphasis and costs got caught up in the inflation resulting from the Spanish-American War. The *Chicago Tribune* did attempt to reinstitute it again in 1910. But in the years 1895 to 1898, the one-cent newspaper had changed Chicago and journalism in ways that inflation could never undo. It had pulled the "back alley" people a little more into the process and helped teach the powerful a little better what the process is.

Newspapers Start Selling for a Penny

1. The *Tribune* in 1883 had editorially attacked "penny journalism," calling it "a great mistake publishers have made" ("The Chicago Tribune: Its First 100 Years" Vol. II, p.55). The editorial continued: "They [papers selling for 2 cents] have in a moment of frenzied rivalry made an excessive reduction and cut down the price of what costs 3 or 4 cents to 2 cents in order to attract a class of readers who do not like the 'high-toned' kind of papers and who would not read them as a gift, and who would add nothing to the value of a newspaper's circulation if they did read it. Quality is worth quite as much in newspaper circulation as quantity. It is a mistake to describe your goods to those who have no money to buy them with."

2. One should not detract from the journalistic genius of Melville Stone and Victor Lawson. Yet, the *Tribune*'s change in 1895 to what they had done for 20 years was a journalistic turning point. The *Tribune* was the "old order" changing. It was almost 50 years old. The paper had helped elect Abraham Lincoln President. It had international prestige (aided by its role in helping to conceive the World's Columbian Exposition), was very smartly edited and carried voluminous advertising. It also was strongly committed to business (often claiming that such a bias was the best thing for the workers). This was the newspaper that went from 3 cents to 2 cents on July 9, 1888 and then dropped to a penny in 1895. After the 1888 drop, it called itself "The People's Own Paper." In 1895, it started taking that concept more seriously.

3. Pennies were scarce in Chicago in 1876 when Stone and Dougherty founded the *Daily News*. They had to "import barrels of pennies from the Philadelphia Mint and persuade certain merchants to mark their goods 59, 69 or 99 cents." This, Stone tells us in his autobiography, "Fifty Years a Journalist" (Doubleday, Page & Co., 1921) p.60 was the beginning of stores marking such prices on merchandize and the mass introduction of the penny into the Midwest. The paper was modeled after the *New York Daily News* and *Philadelphia Star*, both of which had been successful.

4. Chicago in the 1890s was a lively newspaper town. An 1891 *Chicago Guide*, for example, lists: 24 dailies; 260 weeklies; 36 semi-monthlies; 5 bi-monthlies; 14 quarterlies; or 531 total. By the end of the decade, the number climbed to over 600. The more prominent included: the *Daily News*, the *Tribune*, the *Evening Journal*, the *Herald*, the *Inter-Ocean*, the *Times*, the *Post*, the *Abendpost*, the *Arbeiter Zeitung*, the *Globe* and later in the decade, the *Record*.

5. It is often difficult looking back on the history of the *Daily News* to see where recognition of Melville Stone and of Victor Lawson stopped or started. Their biographies don't help. The paper was successful enough to make both of them rich (Lawson, much more so) and to credit both of them. A good history of the era can be found in "Victor Lawson: His Time and His Work" by C. H. Dennis (University of Chicago, 1935).

6. Eugene Field died suddenly in the middle of the night a couple of days before the *Tribune*'s new one-cent price went into effect. His disappearance from the pages of the *News* may have contributed some to the *Tribune*'s sudden gain.

7. "Chicago Tribune, " 1946 p.277

8. James Linn, "James Keeley, Newspaperman," (Bobbs-Merrill, 1937) p.72.

9. Ibid. p.167.

10. One of the places where this Medill misquote appears is on p.68 in Wayne Andrews' "Battle for Chicago" (Harcourt, Brace & Co., 1946). As with other references, no source or date is given to substantiate it. It also appears without citation in "The Media in America" by John Tebbel (Crowell Co., 1974). In the Andrews' version, Medill is quoted as suggesting the benefits of using "strychnine or arsenic" on "tramps." The full quotes and rebuttal appear in Lloyd Wendt's well-researched "Chicago Tribune: The Rise of a Great American Newspaper" (Rand, McNally & Co., 1979) p.570. Also arguing against the validity of the quote is the fact that Medill's editorials did seek positive solutions such as "co-operatives" for the poor and the unemployed. Perhaps, one of the most meaningful critiques of Medill was made by the man whom the *Tribune* had railed against as much as it had against any, the free-thinker, Robert Ingersoll. Upon Medill's death, he said: "For many years he [Medill] was a great power for good. In my opinion, he was the greatest, the most efficient editor in the western states. Mr. Medill lived a useful life and usefulness is the only true religion."

11. "Democracy and Social Ethics," (Macmillan, 1908) p.8.

Chicago Uncovers the American Language

In the Middle Ages, the cultivated of Europe used a different language from the people. It was Latin. That ancient language gave them a universal tongue impervious to both local dialect and the constant changes in the speech of the people. Latin was spoken by the literati, but even more often used for writing their literature and documents.

Throughout the first hundred years of this nation's history, the British language served a similar function. If you were educated or a member of society, you were expected to write and to speak "the King's English" and not let your expressions include dialect or colloquialisms, much less slang. Your language was an absolutely essential passport into elite society.

The British language—kept pure by teachers in the "better" schools—became so entrenched that it is still used in legal and educational documents in its most stifled form. It was a dead language which admitted almost as few changes as did Latin.

Probably the most common term for it was "proper English." Compared to common speech, it was full of abstraction and circumlocution. It had a precision that local dialects with their many variances and changes lacked. And, to the "educated," it was sacred.

The appearance of Abraham Lincoln on the American scene was a cold-water shock to the language of the American elite. He spoke a different tongue than they. He talked as a Midwesterner who had never been given a "proper" education - one received at Harvard, Yale or the prep schools. Lincoln - a decent grammarian - used the language spoken as the dialect of the Midwest.[1] Even when he put it aside as in some of the phrases of the Gettysburg Address such as "Fourscore and seven years ago," his language remained far more common and direct than that of public orators including Edward Everett, who also spoke on the occasion.

The elite in America jealously guarded their language and later formed organizations dedicated to preserving it. It was part of a culture to which people were to be "raised up" rather than to have it be "lowered" to them. In other words, it was not to be popularized or democratized.

Lincoln was chided by his predecessor, former President John Tyler, for affrontery to the "proper" language of the country. Mencken, in his book, "The American Language," states that Lincoln was "unaware" of violating the principles of language so important to those who considered themselves "proper." Lincoln himself said he didn't care "a cornhusk for the literary critics."[2]

Another Midwesterner who put the ax to the British language in this country was Mark Twain, who wrote and spoke directly and simply and often picked up the dialect and blunt language of the people, His wife, however, did at times edit his works to make them more "proper." Other local-color writers such as Bret Harte helped to downplay proper English while pushing in the direction of a polyglot American language.

What America needed was a language of its own[3] that was simple and direct enough to be spoken by the people but universal enough and stable to the extent that it could be American. While founded in the British language, it could admit words from slang as well as from the many nationalities being absorbed into the American culture.[4]

Lincoln pioneered that language, but as the reported not the literary word. A mass effort, supported by tremendous educational tools, would be necessary to make the official, universal language of this nation American rather than proper English or the various accents such as Bostonian, New York, Brooklyn, Southern, Kentuckian, Creole, Hoosier or Texan.

The flowering of American culture in Chicago during the 1890s did it. It universalized the Midwestern dialect made up of the simple direct speech used by Lincoln as well as the Americanized expressions created by the immigrants. Thus a national tongue was molded that became acceptable both for writing and speaking, And, more important, it was a democratic language forged by the people and, to an extent, changeable by them.

In his brilliantly put-together book "The Rise of Chicago as a

Literary Center," Hugh Duncan talks of Chicago's role in establishing the American language.

> When we consider the linguistic habits of Chicago of these years (1875 to 1910), we find that the functions of speech were very different than they were in Boston. The relation of word and thing, or word and action, was far more intimate in Chicago usage than in a society where a usable literary tradition existed, and where images of life were formed in written works. Chicago words and phrases were related to action, and especially the action of the new urban world developing so rapidly after the Civil War. The language of sports, business, politics, and work had to be invented. The writers of the school and studio knew that the newspaper writers such as George Ade and Ring Lardner were creating an indigenous urban language. Howells, Garland, Fuller (as well as Henry James and Henry Adams) realized that Ade's galaxy of Chicago types offered the promise of an indigenous American literature, just as Mark Twain's town and rural characters had given us the indigenous American literature of the rural Middle West. Howells and Fuller begged Ade to do an American novel, just as the "intellectuals" whom Lardner hated begged him to realize himself more fully in "art."[5]

Their impatience, however, went for naught. You cannot rush the birth of a "literary" language anymore than you can that of a child. It wasn't simply "Ade's galaxy" at work on it. Eugene Field's writings were chiseling on it long after his death, as were those of other Chicago journalists and novelists. The railroads were crushing down the barriers and the distance that had given rise to localisms and even accents. The push of Chicago business, the nationalization of sports such as baseball, the innovation of the penny newspaper, the involvement of the poor in politics, the promotional literature of the mail order houses, the words of the syndicated comics and the Americanisms that dominated the lines that flashed on early silent movie screens all helped determine and develop that language.

Our language is called American, but at the time it was more specifically Chicagoese.

This Chicago language did not find all of its roots in the city's boundaries any more than did the grain and hogs that made Chicago famous. The language drew from the same rich Midwestern soil as they. Ade, McCutcheon and others came from Indiana. Eugene Field and Floyd Dell came from the banks of the Mississippi River. Edgar Lee Masters and Vachel Lindsay—to use a localism—hailed from the area around Springfield, Illinois. Carl Sandburg was from Galesburg, Illinois.

The two languages—proper and American—were pitted in a struggle starting in the 1880s that still has not ended. But the most intense developments in favor of the American language took place between 1890 and 1917, and in Chicago. People, especially teachers, chose up sides (the latter expression being an excellent example of the type of Americanisms that were suddenly allowed to enter even the written language of this country.)

Perhaps the second classic battle between America's established literary language and newly emerging one (the first being at Gettysburg, Lincoln versus Edward Everett) was a chance one in 1888. Two new poems appeared in the same issue of a literary magazine, *America*. One was by the most noted living poet and critic in the United States, James Russell Lowell of Cambridge, Massachusetts. The other was by Eugene Field. Both poems became instantly popular and were reprinted in a flood of newspapers. It became a competition to see which would ultimately become the more appreciated. Lowell's poem, written in the traditional language of nineteenth century poetry, was "St. Michael the Weigher." Field's short verse, while not a complete breakaway from proper English, was more in the language of the people. Ultimately, that poem, "Little Boy Blue," won.

Field's friend and biographer Charles Dennis reports that the author was aware of the competition and kept a newspaper clipping file on each and "To Field's immense satisfaction 'Little Boy Blue' soon began to outrun its more pretentious rival."[6]

In comparing the final verses of both poems, we can note that neither man used a word with more than two syllables (except for a hyphenated one in Lowell's). The sharp comparison is in the difference between Lowell's abstract language and Field's use of particulars.

"St. Michael the Weigher" ends:

Marvel through my pulses ran
        Seeing then the beam divine
Swiftly on this hand decline,
        While earth's splendor and renown
Mounted light as thistle-down.

Field's "Little Boy Blue" concludes:

Ay, faithful to Little Boy Blue they stand,
        Each in the same old place,
Awaiting the touch of a little hand,
        The smile of a little face;
And they wonder, as waiting the long years through
        In the dust of that little chair,
What has become of our Little Boy Blue,
        Since he kissed them and put them there.

The two are different poems, but they are also written in different languages. "Little Boy Blue" was not one of Field's more colloquial poems and many "educated" persons might have shunned it if it had contained the contractions, slang and offensive words to the establishment such as "ain't" that were often part of his poetry.

Still, it was more George Ade and Finley Peter Dunne, two other Chicago newspaper columnists, who were to become nationally and internationally famous precisely because of their use of language.

George Ade moved to Chicago in June, 1890 from Indiana and landed a job as a reporter on the *Morning Record*. Within a year and a half he was its star reporter and by 1893 had his own column, called "Stories of the Streets and of the Town." He was soon writing an unprecedented two columns a day. In his own words, he showed a "criminal preference for the Midwest vernacular." His columns became books and he quickly gained national attention, whereupon he was "discovered" by the dean of American literary critics, William Dean Howells.

What Ade did was use the language of the people with a heavy dose of slang. He proved that it could carry emotion, sensitivity and life; he showed, as Damon Runyon later did, that slang could be a beautiful and expressive language. Among those whom he would directly affect would be John McCutcheon, Theodore Dreiser, Finley Peter Dunne, Booth Tarkington and Opie Read.

Even more popular in his era and no less an innovator was Finley Peter Dunne, also a Chicago newspaperman. Dunne created the character Mr. Dooley with all his South Side Irish brogue witticisms such as "Trust ivirybody—but cut the cards." First in Chicago and after 1900 in New York, he was the Will Rogers of his era. His radical break with formal English helped make room for those who wanted to admit dialect and street language in speech, newspapers, poetry and books. [7] He became so popular that students could even quote him in the classroom in defense of their aberrations from the proper language.

Ade, Dunne and their coterie were listeners. They reported the new language but they did not delve deeply into it. Ade, for example, picked up his slang from an office boy at his newspaper and Dunne, his brogue and characters from Chicago saloons he frequented.

The man who grabbed hold of the language and gave it a good shaking was a sports reporter for the *Chicago Tribune*, Ring Lardner. He bored inside the native language of America and reconstructed it in print. The index to H. L. Mencken's "The American Language" is replete with references to Lardner's use of it. Of the sports reporter, Mencken wrote:

> The business of reducing the American language to print had to wait for Ring Lardner, a Chicago newspaper reporter. In his grotesque tales of baseball players, so immediately and so deservedly successful, Lardner reports the common speech not only with humor, but also with utmost accuracy.[8]

In a single story by Lardner, in truth, it is usually possible to discover examples of almost every logical and grammatical peculiarity of the emerging language, and he always resists the temptation to overdo the thing. Here, for example, are a few typical sentences from "The Busher's Honeymoon:"[9]

> I and Florrie was married the day before yesterday just like I told you we was going to be...You was to get married in Bedford, where not nothing is nearly half so

> dear...The sum of what I have wrote down is $29.40...Allen told me I should ought to give the priest $5...I never seen him before...I didn't used to eat no lunch in the playing season except when I knowed I was not going to work...I guess the meals has cost me all together about $1.50, and I have eat very little myself...
>
> I was willing to tell her all about them two poor girls...They must not be no mistake about who is the boss in my house. Some men lets their wife run all over them...Maybe you could of did better if you'd of went at it in a different way. Both her and you is welcome at my house...I never seen so much wine drank in my life...

Ring Lardner was a revolutionary without much of a literary following.10 A few writers in later years, such as Damon Runyon and Jimmy Breslin, columnist for a string of New York papers and author of "The Gang that Couldn't Shoot Straight," were among the few who have attempted to write in the American vernacular.

This failure of writers of subsequent eras to follow up the literary discovery of the American language has been deep tragedy for American society. The refusal to accept and respect the American vernacular has helped to continue the deep chasm between the well-to-do and the poor that was a carry-over from the aristocratic nineteenth century in this century. The "lower" class is given constant reminders that its language is to be considered "inferior" to that of the rest of American society. English in schools is geared to humiliate the vernacular into submission. The result is a deep sense of inferiority on the part of the poor or "uneducated" about their speech and even more their writing.11

It is true that the language of the so-called "lower class" has certain limitations. Such speech can't as precisely express abstraction as can a more "proper" English. It is not as universal as the traditional literary language and is more easily changed by every passing influence.

English teachers to the contrary, however, the American vernacular stands as a valid language. It is often more sensitive and expressive than English, even American English. It is delicately and creatively alive, capable of being the language of poetry and prose as well as speech. There have been exponents of it over recent years and they have been severely criticized for that. No matter what else you might say about one of them, his use of American vernacular (mixed with South Side Chicago Irish), bonded him with large segments of the people. The man was the late Richard J. Daley, "dah mare of Chicawgah."[12] One of his successors, Harold Washington, was noted for the same successful and effective use of the language of the man and woman of the street. For both, it was the ultimate glue in their coalitions.

1. Carl Sandburg in his "The War Years" biography of Lincoln argues that his "plain speech"—contrasted with the aristocratic manner of the South—was considered by contemporary commentators helpful in winning support for the North in Democratic-leaning nations. Cf. Vol. II, the chapter on his speech at Gettysburg. William Herndon, law partner and biographer of Lincoln, repeatedly characterizes Lincoln as "direct in speech."

2. In "The War Years" (Harcourt, Brace & Co., 1939) Vol. II p.305, Sandburg adds:

> The *Boston Transcript* noted his use of "the plain homespun language of a man of the people, who was accustomed to talk with the 'folks'" and "the language of a man of vital common sense, whose words exactly fitted his facts and thoughts."

3. The leading authority on the development of the language of this country is H. L. Mencken's "The American Language" (Alfred A. Knopf, 1919). The book suffered many revisions, principally by the author himself. Unfortunately, as far as an awareness of the vernacular is concerned, these were often dilutions rather than improvements. Both the original and the first revision (1921) were lengthy and eloquent arguments demanding respect for the "American" or common language of the people. By the second revision (1930), we see fewer references in the index, for example, to Abraham Lincoln and Mark Twain. By the time it added substantial supplements in the mid-1940s, it became further watered down while appearing more sophisticated.

4. Language, of course, can be subdivided, especially if one does not emphasize too exactingly the lines separating one division from another. There are: "gutter talk," slang, the "shoulda went" speech, dialect, newspaper or mass media language, "proper English," sophisticated, literate, legal verbiage and cybernetics, to label a few of its forms. The gradation on this list is not based on "correctness" or even precision, but rather on the degree of formalization.

5. "Culture and Democracy" (Bedminster Press, 1965) p.52.

6. Dennis, p.163. Acknowledgedly, "Little Boy Blue" had the advantage of being a heart tugger almost unmatched in literature. The competition between the two poems is also described in "Field Days" by Robert Conrow (Charles Scribner's Sons, 1974) p.183.

7. Hugh Duncan in "Culture and Democracy" (Bedminster, 1965) has a chapter titled "Journalism and the New Urban Speech of Chicago." He quotes Dunne as saying, "When we Americans are through with the English language, it will look as if it had been run over by a musical comedy."

8. Duncan, p.50.

9. "You know Me, Al," (Charles Scribner's Sons, 1916) p.67.

10. Ring Lardner did have a strong readership, however. His column "In the Wake of the News" was devoured by *Chicago Tribune* readers and syndicated throughout the country. His short stories were compiled in six volumes, including "You Know Me, Al," "Gullibles Travels" and "Round Up." He died in 1933. Perhaps, a little of his down-to-earthness can be attributed to surviving the name, Ringgold Wilmer Lardner. His son, Ring, Jr., became a top Hollywood scriptwriter.

11. One of the few areas in life where polyglot American or the vernacular in its many variations is respected and enjoyed in the United States is in sports. A Dizzy Dean, a Casey Stengel, a Leo Durocher or even a Monday night football announcer is forgiven much as long as his language is colorful and something with which people can identify.

12. Mayor Daley could speak quite distinctly and usually did, but when he became either relaxed or frustrated, he slipped into the vernacular. He could also use either form of speech for effect. For a book of Daleyisms, see, "Quotations from Mayor Daley" compiled by Peter Yessne (Pocketbooks, 1969). Harold Washington loved the reaction of a crowd when he used the language they knew was theirs. Ditto for Jesse Jackson.

Chicago, Literary Capital of America

Porkopolis—as the East deridingly called Chicago—was considered a missionary outpost in the cultural world. Author and literary esthete Hobart C. Chatfield-Taylor, who lived in Chicago, placed the number of "true sophisticates" in the city in 1890 at less than 100.

And yet, 27 years later, at the end of the World's Fair generation, the high priest of American culture, H. L. Mencken, called Chicago "The Literary Capital of the United States."

An analogy might describe Chicago as gushing fresh thoughts and feelings into the American mainstream, changing its quality and taste.

Ironically, it was a freshness not unrelated to the infamous Bubbly Creek, a Chicago River tributary, which by 1900 had become the Union Stockyard's cesspool.

The city's odors emanated more distinctly from that creek than from any other spot. The packinghouse lords such as Gustavus Swift regularly visited Bubbly Creek to ascertain the degree of fat and by-products being wasted.

It would be difficult to imagine, especially on a warm day, a Henry Wadsworth Longfellow or an Oscar Wilde being inspired in the same city as Chicago's Bubbly Creek. Still, to the confounding of classicists, Harriet Monroe's genteel *Poetry: a Magazine of Verse* was born in that day and age in Chicago and it first printed Carl Sandburg's *Chicago,* with its refrain "proud to be Hog Butcher...to the nation."[1]

Because of—or despite—the smell in Chicago, H. L. Mencken summarized what had been happening in the world of American literature. In an article that appeared in 1917 in the *Chicago Tribune* and again in a British magazine in 1920, the Baltimore journalist wrote:

> In Chicago there is a mysterious something that makes for individuality, personality and charm. In Chicago, a spirit broods upon the face of the water. Find a writer who is indubitably an American in every pulse-beat, snort and adenoid, an American who has something new and peculiarly American to say and who says it in an unmistakably American way and nine times out of ten you will find that he has some sort of connection with the gargantuan and inordinate abattoir by Lake Michigan—that he was bred there, or got his start there or passed through there in the days when he was young and tender.2

The word "abattoir" is about as fancy a way that he could have found to call the whole city a slaughterhouse.

Mencken, speaking of the great American writers (Fuller, Norris, Dreiser, Herrick, Ferber, Anderson, Sandburg, et al.), continued the metaphor, saying they "reek of Chicago in every line they write." And, he adds, "the city is American in every chitling and sparerib, and it is alive from snout to tail."

The supreme literary compliment that the Baltimore editor handed to the abattoir by the lake was that "in Chicago originality still appears to be put above conformity."

Mencken wrote these words at the zenith of the city's literary fame. Having discharged its all into America's mainstream, Chicago found little in itself to sustain its own unique and separate life. Most of its successful writers either stopped writing or left Chicago.

Although several major writers (Hamlin Garland, Theodore Dreiser, Floyd Dell and Edgar Lee Masters) moved to New York, the majority who left Chicago dispersed much after the manner of the early Christian apostles.

The key to Chicago's thrust and then dissipation was, according to Mencken, that Chicago indeed did have "something new and peculiarly American to say" and found ways to say it in that were "unmistakably American."

Much of what was written and the people who wrote it have been forgotten outside the college classroom, but they deeply altered American literature and culture. They contributed a strangely scarce American commodity—originality.

Literary Capital of America

At the time of the 1893 Columbian Exposition, Chicago had only a minor literary tradition. Kenny Williams has documented it in her book, "Prairie Voices: A Literary History of Chicago from the Frontier to 1893."

Nevertheless, Chicago had been a city in preparation. Literature—as one of the arts—was something to be supported by the wealthy, leisure class. While Chicago had a rapidly growing wealthy class (100 millionaires made their fortune in the city between the Civil War and 1890), there was no leisure class in the city. "Work" was the sound of its heartbeat. It did, however, have something else that could become the stepping stone for the novelist or poet—newspapers.

Many of Chicago's great literary figures came here either to become newspaper reporters or because the papers published their words. Newspapers were the magnet to make Chicago a literary center.

The list of newspaper reporters and editors who created literature in Chicago reads like a Who's Who of the era: Eugene Field, Frances Willard, Henry Demarest Lloyd, George Ade, Theodore Dreiser, Finley Peter Dunne, John T. McCutcheon, Ring Lardner, Carl Sandburg, Ben Hecht and L. Frank Baum.[3]

These are all remembered more for their books than their reporting, but the fact is that the newspaper was literature and many of these writers merely put between covers what they wrote for edition.

As authors of books, they made surprisingly little money, especially at the outset. Chicagoans were reluctant to spend $1 or $1.50 for a book when they could get five or six daily newspapers for one to five cents each. The Chicago papers in the 1890s began serializing popular novels and thereby helped change reading habits. Ultimately, the books of the Chicago writers were for those people not privy to the city's newspapers. And these authors did break through, not only in the United States, but also in Europe.

Frances Willard, who had been a Chicago newspaper editor in the 1870s, wrote some imaginative and thoughtful books, as did *Tribune* editorial writer Henry Demarest Lloyd. Puckish, incisive Eugene Field merrily hoed the fields that many of these would plant in and reap from.

George Ade, however, the day he arrived in Chicago from Brook, Indiana in 1890, became more completely part of what the city was saying than Eugene Field did in the decade he wrote daily columns about Chicago.

Ade, who rose spectacularly from cub reporter to columnist in two years with the *Morning News* and *Chicago Record*, was not the natural humorist that Field was. George Ade was a listener; the language, humor and "message" of Chicago could be heard in his "Stories of the Streets and of the Town," columns (often, two a day)

The speech of George Ade's characters was frequently called "slang." It was a Chicago dialect which he is said to have learned from a newspaper copyboy. In retrospect, he was defensive of it and said, "People in my stories had talked slang, but only when they had to do so in order to be plausible and probable. If I used a word or phrase that was reasonably under suspicion, I would hang up the quotation marks so that the reader might know I was utilizing it for a more picturesque effect."[4]

His defense falls apart when we see he didn't set off the phrase "hang up the quotation marks" in this statement.[5] His language was fresh and original in a literary world that was proudly stilted. He wrote:

> The American must go to England to learn for a dead certainty that he does not speak the English language...one is a pure and limpid stream; the other is a stagnant pool swarming with bacilli.

Ade wrote about ordinary, unpretentious people. He achieved his greatest warmth and humor when the basis of it was contrasting the "proper" with natural, instinctive actions of ordinary people.

Of him, William Dean Howells wrote:

> In Mr. George Ade, the American spirit arrives; arrives, put down its grip, looks around, takes a chair and makes itself at home...the level struck is low: the level of the street...and Mr. Ade would not think of apologizing for the company he invites you to keep.[6]

Finley Peter Dunne, who was Ade's contemporary, is in many ways a literary relic today. He created Mr. Dooley, a character with a heavy brogue and Chicago Irish wit. Chicagoans enjoyed Mr. Dooley's comments first in the *Chicago Evening Post* and, starting in 1897, in the *Chicago Journal*. His observations on Dewey's victory at Manila in 1898 made him a U. S. sensation and obtained a very strong national syndication, making him the pre-eminent American humorist for over a decade. Mr. Dooley was a man of the people, who used their language, but who could never become a true democrat as long as his philosophy was: "Trust ivirybody—but cut the cards." His was not the warm faith of Will Rogers' statement, "I never met a man I didn't like."

Theodore Dreiser, on the other hand, who could be haughty, but was deeply touched by Chicago commonness and expressed it in the realism—and often tenderness—of his writing. He lived in Chicago only a short time, but used it repeatedly as the scene of his novels.

Dreiser—who arrived from Indiana at approximately the same time as George Ade—was not nearly as successful in Chicago as a newspaper reporter, especially at first. His prose was, at times, turgid and heavy and he did not warm to the language as did some of his contemporaries. He had, however, a unique insight into the human being's relationship to urban life.[7] He allowed his characters in novels such as "Sister Carrie" and "The Genius" to be free. That meant, to the abject horror of the New York Society for the Prevention of Vice, that women could have affairs without suffering severe punishment in the plot.

Ring Lardner, the *Chicago Tribune*'s sports columnist, created a character far simpler, an earthy professional baseball rookie who spoke the American vernacular and shared the sentiments of the beer-drinking fan in the stands.

Ben Hecht, on the other hand, was a sensualist. He learned the vibrant, sensual language. He saw Chicago as an experiential or existential city and reported those experiences, often dabbing in a few pinks and purples along with his pastels.

Hecht is noted for being co-author with Charles MacArthur of the frequently revived play about Chicago journalism, "The Front Page." He was also a Chicago newspaper columnist, short story writer, novelist and finally scriptwriter for Hollywood.

Scholars someday will credit Hecht with a heavier role in American literature and be able to point with more authority to doors he opened in American culture. A certain exaggeration in his style holds back the recognition he deserves. It seems almost as though he were irreverent toward writing. He wasn't, as seen by his involvement with Max Bodenheim in the creation and life of "The Chicago Literary Times."

Harry Hansen delightfully describes Ben Hecht as "Pagliacci of the fire escape."[8]

But the writer in whom the democratic spirit and dynamic push of

Chicago most fully culminated was Carl Sandburg: reporter, poet, historian, folk singer, weaver of children's stories and novelist. He once wrote: "The strong men keep coming on" and that best summarized him. Sandburg had been a roustabout and Spanish-American War solder before deciding to go to Lombard College in his birthplace, Galesburg, Illinois. While there, a few of his essays were privately published and he became enamored of ideas and words and their interplay, and more particularly, free verse.

Sandburg, like the Abraham Lincoln in his voluminous biography, was a man who grew. From 1910 to 1912, he was secretary to the socialist mayor of Milwaukee. He subsequently drifted to a job as a reporter on the *Chicago Daily News.*

His idealism had a harshness to it and it comes out in his "Chicago Poems," written in Carl Sandburg's own version of free verse. Walt Whitman had also written "vers libre." He wasn't accepted either, but even his verse was more measured.

The metered, rhyming verse that Sandburg broke away from represented the same precast forms that Louis Sullivan had revolted against in architecture, the didactic method of communication that Francis Parker and John Dewey had discarded in education, and the rigid traditions that Chicago's democratic souls such as Jane Addams, Clarence Darrow and John Peter Altgeld had attempted to replace with spontaneity and originality.

Sandburg preached free verse. Everywhere, he met opposition. His audiences had been taught that poetry had a set meter and it rhymed. Sandburg showed people differently. He spoke the language of the plain people and used exciting words, "strong, homely ones," and that helped. He had an interesting, if not excellent, singing voice and a touch of drama and that helped too.

In the 1920s, he probably did more for American folk music than any man: collecting, singing and popularizing such ballads as "Casey Jones," "Frankie & Johnnie" and "Blow the Man Down." It was an important era in the history of folk music as the music was still being sung by galoots, gandy dancers, migrants and hobos. The music, at the time, was no more respected than were these outcasts of society themselves. In 1927, Sandburg edited and published "The American Songbag," one of the first and still one of the best collections of folk music.

Within Carl Sandburg there burned an angry and, at times, bitter crusader for the workers, who were laboring hard and not finding the way out as he had through writing and its recompenses. His social conscience lost some of its aggressiveness as he grew older and the city became less his workshop, but that awareness would be there in all his writings.

Sandburg followed "Chicago Poems" with a book of verse about prairie life, "Cornhuskers" (1918), and sequeled that with a return to the city in "Smoke and Steel" in 1920. In the meantime, he continued his reporting for the *Chicago Daily News* and incisively covered the city's white-black riots in 1919. The series was published in book form as "The Chicago Race Riots." By 1922, his emphasis had returned more to rural life in "Slabs of the Sunburnt West."

Men with the new dream shared by Sandburg and his fellow Chicago visionaries exercised the option to see life anew. Consequently, they were often not only prolific, but also diversified. Carl Sandburg certainly was both. His next two works were children's books, "Rootabaga Stories" (1922) and "Rootabaga Pigeons" (1923), followed by "Abraham Lincoln: The Prairie Years," (2 vols., 1926).

"The Prairie Years" became the most popular biography in the country and made Carl Sandburg affluent. The book longed for a sequel, and in 1939, he completed it with the four-volume "Abraham Lincoln: The War Years." According to Elmer Gertz, Sandburg's life of Lincoln "is probably the longest biography in the English language. It contains 1,475,000 words. It is longer than the Bible, longer than Shakespeare; but it has the ebb and flow of the tides, the movement of a great symphony. It can be read more easily than the shorter works of others. It captures not only the spirit of the folk hero, Lincoln, his friends and foes; but also has in it the essence of American democracy."[9]

Sandburg followed his Pulitzer Prize biography with a novel covering the American historical experience. It is titled, "Remembrance Rock" (1948). He then wrote his own autobiography, "Always the Young Strangers" (1953).

Another important reporter had begun his writing career in the early 1920s and also used the new American language and journalistic freedom that had been created in Chicago. He was Ernest Hemingway. Sandburg's message, however, would be truly Chicago and more crusadingly democratic than that of this young writer from the Chicago suburb of Oak Park.

Hemingway, however, and to a lesser extent Sandburg and Hecht, were after-products of Chicago's literary climax. The pre-World War I years saw Chicagoan after Chicagoan push the success button as writers and novelists. Among the latter who were not newspaper reporters primarily were: Sherwood Anderson, a man with self-vision in "Marching Men" and "Winesburg, Ohio"; the University of Chicago's Robert Herrick in an exposé of political hypocricy; Edna Ferber about life on the Near North Side of Chicago in "So Big" or gambling in the Loop in "Showboat"; and Clarence Darrow's law partner, Edgar Lee Masters (an almost Sandburg), in his history, "The Tale of Chicago," his poetry, "Spoon River Anthology," and his novels, "Children of the Marketplace" and "Skeeters Kirby." Even Clarence Darrow joined the parade with a novel, "Farmington," as did *Chicago Tribune* co-owner Joseph Medill Patterson in "A Little Brother of the Rich" 10 and literary critic Floyd Dell with "Moon Calf."

Such a list of names seems no longer of much import except to a college professor teaching the development of the novel or the book collector hoarding first editions. Many other Chicago writers were, to a great extent, ephemeral. But, in their day, they brought the Midwest language to America and to the world and they shared those Chicago experiences and scenes that they themselves experientially understood. Among them there was wide diversity both in message and style; yet Chicago's experience was big enough to encompass all their differences.

The novel that was most emphatically Chicago, however, was written by a man who came to the city to study it so he could write the book. It was Upton Sinclair's "The Jungle."

As a novel, Sinclair's exposé about the lives of the men and women who worked in the stockyards both had limitations and was full of excesses. Nevertheless, for sheer force, it is probably not exceeded in Chicago literature. The Lithuanian family of Jurgis Rudkus and his co-workers of every nationality face the conspiracy of the big city and ultimately the millionaire stockyard owners, who encouraged dreams in their workers but kept families from the realization of them. Twenty years earlier these wealthy men had been the heroes of the Chicago writer. With Upton's book and Frank Norris's "The Pit" about manipulation in the Board of Trade and Theodore Dreiser's works, the titans and tycoons had become national villains.

What Chicago's relationship was to writing was disturbing to many scholars and to almost all literary esthetes who considered themselves the guardians of literature. They didn't want common language and street characters, social exposés, taboo-subject novels or free verse. This group did not desire change, and Chicago seemed nothing but that.

These individuals—and they included a multitude of English teachers as well as members of the Eastern literary establishment—were not overwhelmed with pleasure at the founding in 1912 of *Poetry* magazine in Chicago by Harriet Monroe. They were even less enthusiastic as she proceeded to publish in it Vachel Lindsay and such free verse writers as Sandburg and Ezra Pound. The magazine also subsequently published first Joyce Kilmer's often-criticized pious verse, "Trees," as well as the poems of Robert Frost.

Even less popular with her critics was Margaret Anderson, with her magazine *The Little Review*, which she founded. Of it, Harry Hansen wrote:

> Toward the new art the *Little Review* was hospitable and friendly; toward bourgeois tastes and conventions it was hostile and militant; it scorned smug, self-satisfied writing, commonplace standards, ineffective creation...It fought the battle for free verse, for the imagists...and "discovered" half a dozen hopefuls.[11]

Discovering good writers in Chicago, however, was not all that great a feat. There were so many that they formed a number of literary clubs, or more often met in one of the dozen bars in the city frequented by writers. An early one of these was the macabre "Whitecastle Club," founded around 1890 by Chicago journalists. Its props included a coffin and the reputed skull of an early Chicago reprobate. However, the club that most embodied the free spirit of Chicago's literary colony in its slogan was the Dill Pickle Club, which proclaimed:

> We of the Dill Pickle Club believe in everything. We are radicals, pickpockets, second-story men, and thinkers. Some of us practice free love and some medicine. Many of us have tired of our wives.

Chicago during this era, it might be noted, had the largest electric generators in the world, thanks to the demands of the city and the foresight of Samuel Insull. In the year 1917, those mechanical wonders were switched to helping Chicago gear up to be the arsenal of war. The human dynamos of the city, however no longer found a demand for the Chicago message of culture and democracy during the war, only one for propaganda and the spirit of patriotism. The chauvinistic propaganda of the war helped turn the people off to the writers and the era of Chicago the literary capital of the United States was ended.

1. It is as important to understand Chicago as "hog butcher to the world" in this era as it is to recognize biographically that Napoleon was short. In both cases, part of the tremendous inner drive seemed to be an overcompensaton. University of Chicago historian Bessie Louise Pierce's work, "As Others See Chicago" (University of Chicago, 1933) is a collection of impressions of visitors to the city from 1673 to 1933. If there is one repetitious image, it is Chicago as "Porkopolis." Also, Chicago stunk much more in the nineteenth century than in the twentieth, because the river was effectively reversed in 1900 so sewage from the stockyards no longer stagnated in the river and lake.

2. Many authors have attempted to analyze or at least report the literary revolution that took place in Chicago at the turn-of-the-century. One of the most exciting was Hugh Duncan in "Rise of Chicago as a Literary Center from 1885 to 1920" (Bedminster Press, 1964). It is the source for the Mencken quotes. On the other hand, one of the flattest is "Chicago Renaissance, the Literary Life in the Midwest 1900 to 1930" (Appleton Century, 1966). The latter is broad, well-documented and fairly easy reading, but fails to capture a theme to the revolution it reported. Duncan's "Culture and Democracy" (Bedminster, 1965) incorporates material of his other, shorter work, and gives it more of a framework. Kenny William's "In the City of Men" (Townsend Press, 1974) is good on the early part of literary blossoming, while Alson J. Smith "Chicago's Left Bank" (Henry Regnery Co., 1953) is concerned with the latter days of it. Almost every author of the era wrote memoirs...or autobiographical notes. These included Dreiser, Sherwood Anderson, Hecht, Sandburg, Margaret Anderson, Masters and Harriet Monroe. The man who knew many of them and captured their spirits was Harry Hansen in "Midwest Portraits" (Harcourt, Brace & Co., 1923).

3. In the development of this chapter, the author has knowingly omitted a number of important writers in Chicago during the 1890s. These include: Hamlin Garland ("Daughter of the Middle Border", etc.) Hobart Chatfield-Taylor ("With Edge Tools"), Henry Blake Fuller ("With the Procession and "The Cliff-Dwellers"), Robert Herrick ("Gospel of Freedom" and "Chimes"). Nor is a discussion included here of a unique 1890s Chicago literary phenomena, the Stone & Kimball Chap Books. The omission is not based on a lack of literary influence or craftsmenship on the part of any of these. Fuller and Herrick, for example, were expert and significant novelists. However, these were not the writers who "reeked of Chicago in every line they write." In various ways and degrees, they were "Chicago" writers but their audiences tended to be more the city's literati rather than its people. They were not schooled by the same harsh but rewarding taskmaster of the city's democratic surge in the middle 1890s. Garland, for example, fought the vernacular. Chatfield-Taylor dealt with the socially elite, Herrick with campus life and Fuller with the newly rich.

4. A key factor, however, in the development of the Chicago novel was

the change from the 1870s to the 1890s of the price for newspapers to a penny a copy. One of the circulation weapons used, especially by Victor Lawson, was the serialized novel. Other newspapers also used them, but Lawson offered to pay as much as $30,000 for the best serialized mystery stories during this period. Chicago newspaper readers thus became acquainted with the novel and writers found incentive to produce fiction.

5. Ade on George Ade is not the most objective commentator available. His strongest writing was probably his columns written *Chicago Records* during the 1890s with his Stories of the Streets and Town. His reflections came decades later

6. The quote by Howells—who "discovered" Ade as a literary personage—is from the flap of "Chicago Stories" by George Ade (Henry Regnery Co., 1963). The introduction to the book also contains a letter from Mark Twain thanking Howells for introducing him to Geogre Ade's writing and John McCutcheon's illustrations. "Mark", as he signed himself, commented, "My admiration of the book has overflowed all limits, all frontiers...how effortless is the limning. It is as if the work did itself without help of the master's hand."

7. Dreiser's life, like some of his novels, was "tormented," but somehow very compelling. W. A. Swanberg's biography "Dreiser" (Charles Scribner's Sons, 1965) was dedicated to H. L. Mencken, "who knew Dreiser at his best and worst, and fought for the best..."

8. Hansen's warm, literary recognition of Hecht can be found in his book, "Midwest Portraits." The book is also one of the best sources on Sandburg.

9. Gertz's comments are from the Book Bulletin of the Chicago Public Library, Feb., 1948, and were written on the occasion of Sanburg's 70th birthday. Gertz visited Sandburg on the goat farm.in Harbert, Michigan, where the poet had moved. Sandburg subsequently resided in North Carolina, "but in spirit remains the Poet of the Windy City," Gertz wrote.

10. Patterson was one of the most fascinating products of Chicago during this era. The grandson and heir of.Joseph Medill of the Chicago Tribune, he was moved by the Chicago democratic revolution and seemed headed toward a life strongly underpinned by democracy and socialism. He even served under Democratic Mayor Edward Dunne as Chicago public works commissioner, resigning because he considered himself too much of a socialist to hold such a position. In 1919, he founded *The New York Daily News.*

11. Harry Hansen, "Midwest Portraits," p.103.

American Architecture Gets Born in Chicago

One of the strongest and most permanent forces to come out of Chicago just before and after the turn-of-the-century was the non-violent revolution that took place in how we construct buildings, especially the biggest of them

Architecture, before Chicago made its impact, had been the art of aristocrats and kings and an imitative merchant class. On the other hand, Chicago, according to one observer, actually let the "crowd" design the buildings.

It was natural that Chicago, known as the "Mushroom City", should have been a workshop for architecture. After having been almost completely rebuilt following the Chicago Fire of 1871, it then burgeoned over a half a million in population in each of the next three decades.

Land values skyrocketed in Chicago's Loop. As the city spread out, it also became a financial imperative for its core to build upwards. This had become possible because engineers were improving on the elevator that Elisha Graves Otis had invented in 1852. An almost equally important invention burst upon the scene in the middle 1880s in Chicago, the steel skeleton-supported building known as the skyscraper.

Prior to this, the highest a building could hope to be was 10 stories and that was stretching some because the weight of the building rested not on the skeletal structure but on the stone walls. In order for such a building not to collapse, the stone at the base had to be approximately one foot thick for each floor. The formula is fine for pyramids, but has its limitations on a crowded downtown street.

Many architects in the 1870s and 1880s experimented with some use of iron or steel support in buildings. The issue of which was the first skyscraper or steel-skeletal building was not completely settled until 1931. At that time, the Home Insurance Building completed in 1886 at the corner of LaSalle and Adams streets was torn down. A commission of architects ascertained that the weight of the building rested squarely on the steel structure and that, consequently, it had been the world's first skyscraper. The architect had been one of Chicago's most innovative, William Le Baron Jenney.1

The break-through was made. A few additional tall, non-skyscrapers were constructed in the years after 1886 and still stand in Chicago today. The most famous of these is the Monadnock Building at 53 W. Jackson Blvd. There is some use of iron for support. It stands 16 stories, 197 feet tall and is the world's tallest commercial building with outside walls of load-bearing contruction. The north half, designed by John Wellborn Root, was completed in 1891. The south half, by William Holabird and Martin Roche was finished in 1893. The Monadnock made ecologioal innovations in the use of space and air. Its strength was its simplicity.

Justifiably, the name John Wellborn Root and, to a much lesser extent, Daniel Burnham, are attached to the Monadnock Building. Root was climaxing his career (he died in 1891). Burnham was occupied with the World's Columbian Exposition, and hence unavailable to work on the building's second half, if indeed he was capable of doing any such thing without Root. The insistence on simplicity was, however, neither man's, but rather should be credited to Owen F. Aldis, a lawyer and real estate expert, who rejected two of Root's designs for lack of simplicity. He had been equally influential in the design of the Montauk Building (1882) in both cases representing the interests of Peter and Shepard Brooks, entrepreneurs looking for good Chicago investments.2

Many historians cite the desire of such businessmen to put up no-nonsense tall buildings as the driving force in Chicago's simple, direct school of architecture. M. Paul Bourget writing in his book "Outre Mer" in 1893 saw a more basic force loose in Chicago and not elsewhere. Commenting on commercial architecture in the city, he wrote:

> At one moment you have around you only "buildings." They scale the sky with their eighteen, with their twenty stories. The architect who has built, or rather who has plotted them, has renounced colonnades, moldings, classical embellishments. He has frankly

> accepted the condition imposed by the speculator; multiplying as many times as possible the value of the bit of ground at the base in multiplying the supposed offices. It is a problem capable of interesting only an engineer, one would suppose. Nothing of the kind. The simple force of need is such a principle of beauty and these buildings so conspicuously manifest that need that in contemplating them you experience a singular emotion. The sketch appears here of a new kind of art, an art of democracy, made by the crowd and for the crowd, an art of science in which the certainty of natural laws gives to audacities in appearance the most unbridled tranquility of geometrical figures.[3]

In an interesting and insightful commentary on this passage from Bourget, Montgomery Schuyler wrote in 1895:

> It is noteworthy that the observer had seen and described New York before he saw Chicago. The circumstance makes more striking his recognition that it is in Chicago that the type of office building has been most clearly detached and circulated. One is arrested by the averment that this art so evidently made "for the crowd," is also made "by the crowd," since a crowd cannot be an artist, one is inclined to say. But there is not only the general consideration that in architecture an artist cannot even produce without the cooperation of his public, and cannot go on producing without being popular. There is the particular consideration that in this strictly utilitarian building the requirements are imposed with a stringency elsewhere unknown in the same degree, and very greatly to the advantage of the architecture.
>
> Elsewhere, the designer of a business building commonly attempts to persuade or to hoodwink his client into sacrificing utility to "art," and, when he succeeds, it is commonly perceptible that the sacrifice has been in vain and that the building would have been

> better for its artistic purpose if it had been better for its practical purpose. There used to be an absurd story current in New York, of how the owner of two examples of florid classic in cast iron (the Gilsey Building in lower Broadway and the Gilsey House in upper Broadway), exclaimed, when the second was finished, that now he had done enough for art and henceforth he meant to build as a matter of business.
>
> Commercial architecture in Chicago is long past that state, and that it is so is due rather to the businessman than to the architect. In this way and to this extent the architecture is made "by the crowd," it is an architecture of the people and by the people as well as for the people. I asked one of the successful architects of Chicago what would happen if the designer of a commercial building sacrificed the practical availableness of one or more of its stories to the assumed exigencies of architecture, as has often been done in New York and as has been done in several aggravated and conspicuous instances that will readily occur to the reader familiar with recent buildings there. His answer was suggestive: "Why, the word would be passed and he would never get another to do. No, we never try those tricks on our businessmen. They are too wide-awake."[4]

Architectural historians usually choose one of two directions in explaining the evolution of building. They will talk of mechanical inventions and discoveries such as the elevator, improvement in steel, the use of floating caissons or simply the development of the cranes and machines necessary to make them, emphasizing a mechanical determinism. Or else they will stress the vision of a few men and tell how the machines and inventions were forged to make those dreams reality.

Actually, both views can be justified and the most successful architectural firms usually had the artist and the engineer as partners. Burnham was Root's administrative genius and Dankmar Adler was the hard, practical side of Louis Sullivan. Adler was the engineer.

Chicago architects in the 1880s were working out the tough structural problems of foundations, skeletons, use of steel, and what it takes to keep it all together. Some large buildings had crumbled to the ground a year or two after they were built in the early part of the decade. And the designers found the solution often lay in more simple construction.

Once these problems were settled, Chicago needed to state in philosophical terms the meaning of the new architecture it had created. The reason was to simplify and to encourage future designers and architects to grasp this simple architecture as a good one and to avoid the pitfalls and self-delusion of esoteric ornamentation.

And a man to serve this philosophical function stood right up and volunteered. He was Louis Sullivan, who—as a result—has since become known as the "prophet" or "father" of modern architecture.

Sullivan, in many ways, would be outshone by his disciple, Frank Lloyd Wright, and nowhere near receive the public acclaim given to Daniel Burnham. But still, history records him the as first and most complete "American architect."5

Louis Sullivan went from architect-designer to visionary in the early 189Os as the result of an almost mystic experience he had in the middle of a woods where he spent a leave from his work for several months.6 His sense of nature and form came from the lines and images there that impressed him so deeply. Pillars and trees became unified as did vines and architectural ornamentation. But, more than anything else, he gained a simple, honest functionalism that he integrated and made the basis of his concept of architecture.

"Form follows function," Sullivan cried in a voice loud and clear enough for every architect to come after him to have heard and either to have taken into account or deliberately to have ignored.

But what did Sullivan mean? Was it simply another way of telling architects to be as pragmatic as possible? Or was he expressing—as he himself claimed—something deeply democratic and truly religious?

Sullivan wrote two key books that expressed his radical ideas. They were his famous "The Autobiography of an Idea" and the even more inspired "Kindergarten Chats." Neither appeared in book form until after his death in the 1920's, by which time his own creative powers had waned and his life had dissipated, partially due to alcohol.7 But those ideas were read first by architects in what he had designed. Four of his works in particular were as strong in architecture as Patrick Henry's "Give me liberty or give me death" was in the course of American politics.

Sullivan returned from his "retreat" in the woods near Ocean Springs, Mississippi, in March, 1890. A year before, he was the architectural master who, with Dankmar Adler, had completed the poetic culmination of 1880s architecture, the Chicago Auditorium. Now, Sullivan saw himself as more. He was a prophet who had been to the mountain.

The first of his new designs was a tomb in Graceland Cemetery, commissioned by Henry Harrison Getty for his family. Frank Lloyd Wright, strongly influenced by Sullivan's work during this period, later called the Getty Tomb a "requiem in architecture." Its forms and lines were drawn together like the notes of a musical piece.8

And yet, the Getty Tomb does not come across with the bold stroke of a Frank Lloyd Wright house or other example of simple, direct modern architecture. Sullivan was orchestrating in the most refined sense of the word. It is his notes—form and lines—that are simple, not the final product.

Graceland Cemetery's lanes are lined with the tombs and monuments of the wealthy Chicagoans of the late 18OOs. Others try, but none of them—with the exception of Loredo Taft's statue of "Death"—is like the Getty Tomb, a vital statement of life and death. Sullivan's work is genuinely a building that serenely houses the dead and raises questions about life.

His design of the Schlesinger and Mayer Co. store (now Carson Pirie Scott & Co.) on State Street in the Loop went in a different direction. In contrast, another architect might have discovered a "pleasing" and successful ornamentation in designing the tomb and then have tried to repeat it in the store. The thought would have horrified Sullivan who argued that the building's "forms" and designs had to come from its "store" function. Designed and built between 1889 and 1893, Carson's is recognized today as a masterpiece. It was enlarged in 1904 and again in 1960, with the architects respecting his design.

The "form" and "function" of his famous ornamentation on the facade was to showcase the store's display windows. He first considered what would be shown in those windows and for whom it would be displayed before he let those projections determine the lines and forms. Sullivan would nave preferred the word "organic" to describe the relationship between the ornamentation, structure and purpose of the building.

With few exceptions, other architects at the time were unable to see what Sullivan was attempting or even to understand what he was stating. His Transportation Building was considered out of place at the

World's Columbian Exposition. Sullivan, for example, could not refrain from the use of color: it was integral to his work. He looked to the concept of transportation for his design rather than the models of Rome and Greece, as New York architects had. His design won medals from the "Union Central des Arts Decoratifs," the only building at the fair to win foreign honors.

Again, Sullivan in this period did the Schiller Building (1891-92) and later the Garrick Theater (1892). The theater's arched proscenium was probably as clear and strong as any design he conceived. The theater was later torn down to make way for a parking lot, but the statement in stone had been firmly and eloquently made.

Sullivan died in 1924, little appreciated, a man who was recognized as having asked questions, but whose drive for a revolution had failed. Today, his acorns have become oaks and his concepts are acknowledged as underlying what is vital in American architecture. As a result, an architect who would attempt to recreate the acropolis in the middle of an American city would be ridiculed. Gas stations and churches and hamburger stands often try to hide their true functions in elaborate shells, but for the most part public and the larger commercial buildings are not allowed to get away with such deception.

Ultimately, it was Sullivan the teacher even more than the architect who won the victory. His commissions were few in the last two decades of his life, but his writings have reached the young architects who followed him.

Sullivan's basic message was about democracy. He himself said so. And yet it is difficult to look at the highly ornate Carson Pirie Scott & Co. building and immediately see how its design is related to a democratic way of life.

Still, the architect's message comes through in his works as well as his words. When the Chicago Auditorium was re-opened in the late 1960s, required dress for anyone on the first floor was formal tuxedo and floor length gown. Yet, such catering to formality was not the intent of the architects whose masterpiece was being honored. The building was designed for the people. There are only a token number of box seats and the acoustics and seating patterns were deliberately constructed to give optimum benefit to the person holding the cheapest seat. Sullivan and Adler pushed themselves beyond human endurance to make it a hall for the people of Chicago.

His Transportation Building stands out in contrast to the aristocratic conceptualization of the World's Columbian Exposition with its white and classical design. The passages from "The Autobiography of an Idea" (quoted in chapter II) show how insidious he found the idea of elitist architecture. On the other hand, he did not go to the "crowd" to find a design for his buildings. He felt that if a building were going to be functional in society then its design should serve that same function. Therein he participated in democracy.

Significantly, Sullivan did not limit his concept of form and function to architecture. He used it also in his writing, very often with striking success. His most famous work is often considered to be about his own life. The title is "The Autobiography of an Idea." In it, Sullivan speaks of himself in the third person. He wants the idea rather than the author of the book to be in the first person. His other major work, a compilation of 52 essays, appeared in 1901 in *Interstate Architect and Builder*. They were written in the very informal peripatetic form in which a master architect and his student walk through the Chicago Loop and discuss architecture, democracy, education, the modern city and the specific buildings. The teacher often heaps scorn upon both the architecture and the pupil's schooling.

"The Autobiography of an Idea" sees architecture "as a spiritualization of function and form which must both mirror and organize the social and cultural forces of each epoch."

Few people, even among architects, see the art of building as so basic, so central to life. Unfortunately, it is often those who create the designs and determine the shape of structures who have the least sense of architecture's function as envisioned by Sullivan.

To Louis Sullivan, architecture was the cradle in which the child is placed, the log cabin in which the wilderness is mastered, the church in which we look into our souls, the school in which we entrust learning, the bakery in which we make bread, the store in which we sell goods and the tomb in which the body is put aside. He looks into these functions of architecture for their forms, their essences and asks engineers, craftsmen and workers to create buildings that are true to those inner purposes.

In "The Autobiography of an Idea" he told us how that idea grew into a virtual force in the man, Louis Sullivan. The story of the book, although published in 1924, ends time-wise where modern architecture is said by many to have begun, at the 1893 World's Columbian Exposition, when Sullivan designed the Transportation Building.

Claude Bragdon, in the introduction to the book, wrote: "With no disparagement to his achievements as architect and designer, I hold that Louis Sullivan makes his most powerful and lasting appeal as author and teacher."

Frank Lloyd Wright referred to Sullivan simply as "der Meister."

Yet, it was in his lesser known work, "Kindergarten Chats,"9 that Louis Sullivan showed his full power as a teacher. Through the words of the pupil in the book, he is repeatedly able to portray the pedantic thoughts in life that we all tolerate in ourselves until we run into the vision of a teacher such as Sullivan.

The master, for example, is willing to accept the pupil's view that a bank can be designed like a Roman temple and be attractive. Sullivan's proposed qualifications are then that "the banker wear a toga and sandals and conduct his business in the venerated Latin language, oral and written." He also suggests anyone who wants to build such a bank should do it in his own backyard and "not on the people's highway and label it modern architecture."

Sullivan's sarcasm becomes near ecstatic when he describes a scheme by Detroit officials to erect the tallest Doric column in the world to commemorate the city's bicentennial. He said, "I particularly detest wanton, expensive humbug...even if it is not specifically the largest in the world." He saw no relation between the lives and visions of the early settlers and the Doric column. He called it an "inhuman response."

He figuratively loaded his shotgun took aim and shot at the buildings some of his fellow Chicago architects had created. One he described as "an ill-compounded salad, with a rather rancid New-Yorkey flavor." He gets irate over a department store that looks more like a hotel and calls it "canting and hypocritical, to couch our definition in the mildest terms."

Then he pulled the other trigger and described the building as "Not characteristic of the West. It lacks utterly western frankness, directness—crudity, if you will. It is merely a well-rooted cutting from the Eastern hot-house and it languishes pitifully in the open air. An expert gardener would not have done so foolish a thing."

He attacks those who say that because something looks "nice" it is good architecture. Sullivan said, "The buildings are there, for good or for evil; they cannot run away; they cannot conveniently avoid investigation." As for those who dismiss differences in architecture as a matter of taste, he says: "Taste is one of the weaker and less significant words in our language. It means a little less than something, a little more than nothing, certainly it conveys no suggestion of potency."

Sullivan's criticism is matched by his praise as he describes a building (the Marshall Field Warehouse) that he saw as "massive, dignified and simple."10 His specific description of it is poetic:

> Four-square and brown it stands, in physical fact a monument to trade, to the organized commercial spirit, to the power and progress of the age, to the strength and resource of individuality and force of character;spiritually, it stands as the index of a mind large enough to cope with these things, master them, absorb them and give them forth impressed with the stamp of large and forceful personality; artistically it stands as the oration of one who knows well how to choose his words, who has something to say and says it.11

Ultimately, Louis Sullivan's yardstick was the one shared by John Peter Altgeld, Jane Addams, Clarence Darrow, Francis Parker, Carl Sandburg and the other great Chicagoans of his era. It was democracy. He saw it as the inner force that must be released from the encumbrances that man and not nature can place on things, on growth and on himself.

Sullivan's statement of what he sees democracy to be, for sheer power, ranks with the most eloquent of his buildings. It appears in "Kindergarten Chats:"

> Democracy is primarily of the individual! It is not a mere political fabric, a form of government; that is but on phase of it—an incidental phase.
>
> Democracy is a moral principle, a spiritual law, a profound subjective reality in the realm of man's spirit. It is an aspiring power whose roots run deep down into those primal forces that have caused man to arise from the elements of earth, and, slowly, slowly through the ages, to assume a rectitude and poise that are of man and of man alone. Democracy is a cast, slowly urging

impulse which, little by little, is exalting man in spirit, and imparting to him the clear definition of his own true image.

Just as man was ages upon ages in learning to stand upon his feet in a physical sense; and just as this accomplishment was the work of a force persistently seeking such expression, so is there an impulse ever at work, ever tending to imbue him with the power to stand upon his feet, morally, and this force we call democracy: It is of that deeply vital impulse of nature which tends ever toward perfecting the type and the individuals of the type, until such time as that impulse shall have spent its force in consumation.

Democracy is not, as you may infer from superficial observation, a merely modern, new-fangled notion of a government of, by and for the people, it is a force, latent and old as earth, a force for whose fulfillment the ages—have been preparing the way, dissolving the obstructions one by one, and slowly making for it a pathway. It is the quiet, the serene forces of nature that are the most powerful; and that force which we call democracy, lying inexpressibly deep-down in the heart and the spirit of man, is seeking, ever seeking its expression.

When the spirit of man first discerned the One Infinite Spirit was the way prepared which must and did lead to the discovery of man by man as himself a god. These discoveries were made by a profoundly contemplative people, and have become our priceless heritage. The latter is credited to the Great Nazarene, who in this sense, was the first democrat. Coming into a world crushed under the heel of absolutism, he spoke to the lowly; he taught that the individual possessed his individual soul. For these and other sayings equally in opposition to the established spirit of his times he was promptly crucified. But his doctrine has survived him, because it is the utterance, not of a man, but of the Infinite Creative Spirit, expressing itself through an overwhelming urgency in nature which found, through this man, a natural and long-sought outlet, doubtless, which nature, through the ages, also had been preparing for itself, in the evolution of those forces which consummated in that man.

So came the truth of democracy into the world of man; and silently it has moved upon its way, through the centuries, a potent aspiring force for the upbuilding of the race. It grows with cumulative power, and, in our land, is seeking and will find its consumation.

Yet, singularly enough, democracy, once a unitary conception of imposing grandeur, in its beauty of divinity in humanity, has subdivided into three separate conceptions; of government, religion and morals. This doubtless is explainable sufficiently by the record of the conflicting interests and forces, political, sacerdotal, and ethical, through which it has sought to express itself or by which such expression has been restrained, diverted, perverted and suppressed.

Yet, clearly, in our land today, we may perceive the varied but powerful currents which are again dissolving these broken thoughts and are bearing them together to form a synthesis which shall define democracy as that high estate which holds in a single conception of CONDUCT, as in a spiritual solvent, the great forces of religion, morals, and government. And this is the conception of democracy that I hold.12

1. Each chapter in this book deserves an adequate and, in most cases, lengthy bibliography. This one, however, has a bookstore all for itself. It's the Prairie Avenue Bookstore. The couple who own it sell books on architecture and on the city of Chicago, but most especially on the Chicago School of Architecture. The variety and amount of literature on the subject is impressive; but most important, this store and the Chicago Historical Society's bookstore at North Avenue and Clark Street are where one has the greatest chance to find a copy of the most exciting books on the subject, Louis Sullivan's "Autobiography of an Idea" (American Institute of Architects, 1924 or Dover, 1956) and "Kindergarten Chats." Also availible are John Wellborn Root's "The Meanings of Architecture" and Frank Lloyd Wright's "The Future of Architecture." These are the important first-person books.

2. The skyscraper and Chicago buildings in general have two particularly good historians in Carl Condit and Frank Randall. Condit's early, famous work was "The Rise of the Skyscraper" followed by "The Chicago School of Architecture," and the two-volume set (published by the University of Chicago Press) "Chicago: 1910-29" and "Chicago 1930-70." The latter are particularly important. Randall's scarce 1949 book is "History of the Development of Building Construction in Chicago."

3. Not many writers on Chicago architecture pick up the importance of Owen Aldis. Harriet Monroe in her biography of her brother-in-law "John Wellington Root" mentioned him several times, but very incidentally. Hugh Duncan and Frank Randall didn't even footnote him. Condit, however, established his influence by quoting his correspondence with the architects.

4. Paul Bourget's book is subtitled "Impressions of America." It is critical of "the high pitch and intensity of America's lifestyle." However, Bourget's writing style itself seems quite intense. The quote here is from Montgomery Schuyler's article. Cf. following footnote.

5. The quote is from an article in December 1895 *Architectural Record*. The piece was reprinted in Vol XII, p.53, of "The Annals of America" (Encyclopaedia Britannica, 1968). Montgomery Schuyler was an architectural critic and founder of the magazine.

6. Frank Lloyd Wright wrote of the Chicago Architects, "Of them the only men indicating genius above engineering ability and the capabilities of front-men were Louis Sullivan and John Root." These and his additional comments on the two architects are from "A Testament."

7. Claude Bragdon in his "retrospect" at the end of Sullivan's "The Autobiography of an Idea" explains the meaning of the 1890 Ocean Springs "metamorphosis." He states, "T'was here he saw the flow of life, that all life became a flowing for him." Sullivan himself emphasizes how much influence his youth had on his vision and credits John Wellborn Root, a "THINKER," with

the "theory of suppressed functions." Root, Sullivan said, "was as familiar with the great philosophers as with the daily newspapers." While Root with his great talents, was at times "indolent" and "vain," Sullivan—the mystic and democrat—was still his listener. The very use of the word "function" by Root "lit up his [Sullivan's] inner and outer world as one." In these passages from "The Autobiography of an Idea," Sullivan refers to his fellow architect as "John" without using his last name.

8. Disciples and biographers of Sullivan do not make much of a point of alcoholism as a factor in his later life. There were other conflicts that tore him. The discouragement of being a visionary might have been his greatest affliction. On the other hand, some of his associates stayed with his firm long after it was reasonable to do so. His friends rushed the proofs of the autobiography so he could see a copy on his deathbed. His inability to get it published had been one of his great frustrations. A tender account of Frank Lloyd Wright's visit to Sullivan's deathbed appears in Duncan's "Culture and Democracy" (p.461). The book swirls around Sullivan's life and ideas.

9. The Getty Tomb compares dramatically with such other Graceland works as the Potter Palmer's Grecian temple monument that bespeaks wealth and aristocracy, with brewer Peter Schoenhofer's 20-foot high pyramid for himself, with National Baseball League founder William Hulbert's baseball gravestone and with the monument in nearby Rosehill Cemetery for George B. Armstrong of a mail sorting railroad car.

10. "Kindergarten Chats" is a forbidding name for a book and yet is a powerful, visionary work. The misfortune was that it was edited by the publishers to protect readers from "then-current slang," from "most of the puns and such witticisms as seemed forced or unfunny," from "the violence of its invectives" and from "repetitions, redundancies, irrelevances, and digressions." All of these things, along with Louis Sullivan, however, readers might have been able to endure and possibly even appreciate.

11. The Marshall Field Wholesale Store was designed by Henry Hobson Richardson in 1885 and torn down in 1930. Adler and Sullivan's Auditorium Building (now the Auditorium and Roosevelt University) was modeled after it.

12. "Kindergarten Chats" (Dover, 1979) p.30.

Chicago Embraces the Impressionists

Bertha Honore Palmer...

The monument for her and her husband Potter Palmer is the biggest in Graceland Cemetery and in the city of Chicago. It is exquisite classical architecture, simple and white, yet regal with its tall pillars, European, not Chicago.

Yet, of art, she once said:

> What is art? I cannot argue with Loredo Taft who is a pundit, but in my limited conception it is the work of some genius graced with extraordinary proclivities not given to ordinary mortals. Speaking of art...my husband can spit over a freight car.

The woman who made that statement was the hostess to the royalty of Europe at the world's fair and the queen of Chicago society from the 1870s until World War I. She was one of the city's transitional personalities, aristocratic and yet democratic. Like Eugene Field she embodied and promoted much that was Chicago and yet, unlike Jane Addams, she could not always follow through on the consequences of what Chicago was preaching about equality.

For a dozen years, Jane Addams and Bertha Palmer, the social conscience and the social queen of Chicago, were good friends. The Hull House founder on occasion stayed at the Palmer residence and the Chicago society leader used her influence to get Jane Addams elected to the Jury of International Awards at the Paris Exposition in 1900. Jane was the only woman on the prestigious jury. Still, Bertha Palmer broke with Jane Addams when the latter visited an anarchist in jail in 1901. The man was popularly believed connected with the assassination of President McKinley and was having his most basic rights denied, but was later determined innocent and released.

Bertha Palmer, in her Chicagoness, made a contribution to the world in several ways, not the least of which was her help in "discovering" French impressionism.

Her other accomplishments included fighting for women's rights on a world scale and a concern for working women expressed through her involvement in the Columbian Exposition.

Actually French impressionism didn't have to be "discovered" in the late 1880s when Bertha Palmer became interested. It rather needed acceptance, respectability and patronage. As a school of painting in Paris—in the sense of a group of painters who closely followed similar techniques and rules—it was ending in 1886. But, without support, it would have become a fading memory of the progress of art rather than a pillar of it. The dynamic Edouard Manet had died in 1883. Those with whom he had met in the Cafe Guerbois—Degas, Cezanne, Renoir, Monet and others—were beginning to develop something uniquely their own.

> These painters, however, well into the 1890s were treated as revolutionaries who were attempting to destroy art. Impressionism was a bad word, a very bad word.

Writing for *Encyclopaedia Britannica,* Louvre Director Jamot recalled:

> Violent press campaigns little by little inspired the public with horror, disgust and even a kind of incredible hatred for the young (impressionistic) artists. The argument was that they ignored the first rudiments of the art of painting and they themselves were "coarse, extravagant, unconventional Bohemians".1

They indeed could have had all of those vices and still have fit in Bertha Palmer's description of art. Had they possessed them, they would still have found a welcome in Chicago, which was also accused of the same traits.2

French impressionism represented a turning point in art and, in that sense, was revolutionary. Every generation has its young changers and the bigger the change they offer, the stronger are they ridiculed and hated, as for example were the beatniks or representatives of long-haired rock culture of the 1960s.

Also, art in the late 1800s was becoming the living treasury of France. Corot, Ingrès, Millet, Courbet, Rousseau, and the "Academicians" had established a great heritage and respect for painting, They stayed enough within the "tradition" of painting so that they could be accepted and mingled in collections with the classical and neo-classical painters of other countries.[3]

The American art "world" was rapidly becoming a determining factor in the art scene as millionaires were being made overnight and then shipping off to Europe in the morning to buy art. One man, whom they were imitating and who had managed to make money a hundred times faster than they, was saying that patronizing art—not pulling in the money—was what is important. He was Andrew Carnegie.

The steel manufacturer, who bought and preached the merits of such French artists as Corot, Rousseau, Millet, Dupre and Daubigny, refused even to mention the French impressionists or their school in the chapter about art in his book, "Triumphant Democracy." It was published in 1886 and revised in 1893. He certainly mentioned them by inference, however, in describing the effect of the impressionists on current American art:

> Would that my conscience would permit me to leave the subject of American painting without an expression of heartfelt regret that this new art society is far too much French—Frenchy. The recent exhibition, in the words of a true patron of art, "was almost as bad as the Salon—the subjects as a rule unworthy, the landscapes blurred and sketchy, and the nude vulgar.
>
> One consolation remains. These young Frenchy Americans are to be taught another needed lesson. The picture lover and the picture buyer, offended at such a display, will evince his displeasure by showing the value, or rather the no-value, he places upon works which attempt thus to prostitute art to vulgar and unholy ends. If art is to devote itself to the perpetuation of aught but what is noble and pure, may we never be cursed by possessing it. Thank the fates, American literature so far is pure.[4]

And Carnegie was right about impressionism. It was not "holy" in the connotations often given to that word. It was openly sensuous, brighter in color than any painting style ever before and a break with the traditions of lines and space to the point where the painting became "blurred and sketchy." The impressionists probed the artistic freedom that men like Carnegie could not tolerate.

And the steel magnate was not alone. Efforts were made to keep them out of major exhibitions. It wasn't difficult, because not many American millionaires were buying the paintings.

Claude Monet (1840-1926) was one of the chief founders and the most complete protagonist of the French impressionist movement. In 1891, Bertha Palmer, wife of Chicago's prominent hotel keeper and one of its biggest real estate owners, was introduced to Monet in France through her American artist friends, Mary Cassatt and Sarah Hallowell. In the next year, 1892, she bought 22 Monet paintings. Her first Monet cost her $1,000 and her first Renoir $1,700 at a time when a more traditional Meissonier was getting $66,000.

Two other factors occurred simultaneously to make this encounter and these acquisitions important to the history of art. Bertha Palmer was president of the Board of Lady Managers of the World's Columbian Exposition of 1893. And the Art Institute of Chicago's building on Michigan Avenue was erected in preparation for the occasion.

Despite opposition, she managed to get the French impressionists exhibited at the 1893 event. The official French art show at the fair proved the lack of respect shown the impressionists in their own country, That exhibit included only one impressionist painting.

Using Mary Cassatt and Sarah Hallowell to collect paintings on loan to the exposition and borrowing from her own growing collection, Bertha Palmer took the paintings of Degas, Manet, Monet, Pissaro, Renoir, Sisley, and Cazin as well as the more traditional Corot into the halls of the fair. They were a sensation and controversial but were seen by so many that they took hold. She and her husband belonged to almost every art society in the country and her taste meant very much to other collectors, especially the Chicago ones.[5] Locally, Mr. and Mrs. Martin Ryerson collected 13 Monets (including the "Old St. Lazare Station, Paris") and 6 Renoirs (among them "Lady at the Piano" and "Bullfight"). Also, Mrs. Lewis Larned Coburn amassed 6 Monets (one of them "Pool of Water Lilies"), several Renoirs, 2 Manets, a Sisley, and others.

The leading collector, however, remained Bertha Palmer. Her Lake Shore Drive castle-shaped mansion was crowded with art. The paintings were displayed in three tiers and were grouped according to schools.

Probably the Palmers' most loved painting has been "Dans le Cirque" by Renoir. It has appeared in art books without end and sometimes simply in books meant to delight children or to project beauty. It was Bertha Palmer's favorite. She paid $1,750 for it and it is judged to be worth millions of dollars today. Altogether she could count 32 Monets (most prominent of which was "Argenteuil-sur-Seine"), 4 Sisleys, 6 Pissarros, 11 Renoirs, Cazin's "Judith" and the works of other impressionist as well as other post-impressionist painters.[6]

Still other Chicagoans, most notable of which were the Art Institute itself and millionaires such as Frederick Bartlett, took with her the logical next step of acquiring post-impressionist painters such as Cezanne, Gauguin, Van Gogh, Toulouse-Lautrec and Seurat and their successors Matisse, Roualt and Picasso. It was through Bartlett that Chicago acquired its extremely delightful pointillism masterpiece, Seurat's "Sunday Afternoon on the Island of La Grande Jatte."

The collections of the Palmers as well as of the rest of the Chicago millionaires for the most part were willed to the Art Institute of Chicago.[7] Consequently, when any book is put together on the history of paintings, it is usually heavy with acknowledgements to the Art Institute of Chicago in the sections on impressionist—and to a lesser degree, post-impressionism.

Simply amassing numbers or even quality in paintings, however, should not be mixed up with Chicago's principal contribution to the art world. The city—principally Bertha Palmer—made certain that Carnegie's desire to bury what he felt was "Frenchy," "unholy" and "blurred" painting was not fulfilled. The art world was not taught the lesson this super-wealthy mogul wanted to teach it, and the revolution continued.

The turn-of-the-century represented an era for artists in Chicago, one fortunately documented by writer-artist Ralph Fletcher Seymour and commentator Alson J. Smith. In 1898, Seymour arrived in Chicago from a small town in Indiana, seeking work as a commercial artist. He described the very productive environment he found:

> In the early '80s, an unexpected development of the arts appeared in the mid-western country of which Chicago is the heart. Some of the artist-citizens seemed to become aware of the vitality of their surroundings, recognized the brand of living in their neighborhood as peculiarly American, and undertook to translate their understanding of its beauty and meaning into art forms. They believed that art which would interest those around them would have to be expressed in terms of a home-grown, native art. They thought it reasonable that an Indian song sung to Indians meant more to the listeners than the loveliest Brahms song and that art was best understood and of most use to people where it was created. They therefore felt no necessity for turning to European, eastern or conventional rules for guidance in saying what they wanted to say, nor interested in writing in a manner similar to that of Thackery, painting in the classical mode of the French School or erect buildings in the Renaissance style. They wrote and sang of the Great Spirit which was within western men, and voiced enthusiasm for the dangers and hardships natural to the subduing of a continent. They saw the beauty and power in every thing around them. The land was opulent, the men and women living on it resourceful, resolute, creators of their own economic development and ready to create whatever they could use of culture. The artists became popular with the home folks and before long they established the first general expression of a native art in this part of the country.[8]

Smith named names in his chapter titled, "Artist in Porkopolis:"

> The Golden Age of Chicago letters...was also the Golden Age of Chicago art. While Dreiser, Sherwood Anderson, Hecht, Sandburg and Margaret Anderson were embellishing American belles-lettres with their imperishable verbiage, artists like Jerome Blum, Joseph Allworthy, Antony Angarola and Emil Arnim,

> and sculptors of the calibre of Stanley Szukalski and Carl Hallsthammar were following the post-impressionist flag to glory, if not to gold.[9]

"Blum," he called "the Mid-West Gauguin, finding inspiration in Chicago, rather than Tahiti, and splashing his canvases with bold, flowing color."

Angarola, who prematurely died in 1929, was noted for his portraits as well as his habit of lying prone on the floor of the Art Institute to observe certain paintings better.

Ben Hecht described sculptor Stanley Szukalski in "A Child of the Century:"

> Szukalski became a great artist, not only to me, but to a nation [Poland] that was to hail him as the greatest of living artists. Yet his name is today unknown. His works are vanished. He is without public, without critics, and so complete is the world's ignorance of him that he may as well never have existed.[10]

The destruction of Szukalski's works was part of a cosmic event. He had returned to Poland, where the people built an art museum to house and honor his works. It was completely destroyed in the Nazi Luftwaffe bombardment of Poland in 1939.

Among the artists who came out of or studied in Chicago at this time were: Georgia O'Keeffe, whose majestic skies, bold flowers and Southwest vistas stunned the art world; John Vanderpoel, who taught O'Keeffe in 1906 at the Art Institute; Joseph Leyendecker, whose first fame came from illustrating dime novels; Maxfield Parish, the internationally respected illustrator who started in Chicago; Jules Guerin, whose extraordinary drawings illustrate "The Chicago Plan of 1929;" W. W. Denslow, whose zesty drawings illustrate the early Wizard of Oz books; and John T. McCutcheon, who illustrated George Ade's works and whose work, "An Indian Summer," done for the *Chicago Tribune*, has become an American classic.

1. The pivot of the fortune of the school can be found in its 1877 exhibition in Paris. It was here, according to Lloyd Goodrich in *The Arts*, (January 1927) that the group adopted the name, "the impressionists," which had been flung at them. The Goodrich article commemorated the 50th anniversary of that exhibition. At the 1877 exhibition the painters met unprecedented ridicule, but Goodrich adds "from then on conditions began to improve gradually."

2. Mary Cassatt exhibited with the impressionists at the next showing in 1879, the only American to do so. A biography of her traces the history of the group and of her influence on American collectors such as Bertha Palmer and other Chicagoans. It is "Mary Cassatt" by Nancy Hale (Doubleday, 1975).

3. One of the reasons for the almost violent reaction of the French artistic establishment against the impressionists is that they as a group had dared to bypass the established exhibitions or salons that were tightly controlled and were very conservative.

4. Quoted, "The Annals of America," Vol. II, p.95..

5. Bertha Palmer was not without a highly garish Victorian taste. Her castle or mansion on Lake Shore Drive was a monstrosity. It was a turreted, out-of-place remnant of Tudor England. No door had an outside handle, and even the Palmers had to be admitted by servants.

6. The count of paintings is from the chapter on her art collecting in her biography, "Silhouette in Diamonds" by Isabel Ross (Harper & Brothers, 1960). See also: "Chicago Pioneered in Paintings," *Vogue*, August, 1944.

7. She willed that $100,000 worth of her paintings be selected by her sons and given to the Art Institute. She died in 1918. The major portion of the Palmer collection was acquired by the Art Institute in 1922. It included two Delacroix, two Corots, Degas' "Morning Bath," Manet's "Race Track Near Paris," three Pissarros, four Renoirs and seven Monets, according to Frederick Sweet in *Apollo* magazine Sept., 1966. He points out that the "great Chicago collectors" did not buy them for the public, but, as did the Palmers, bequeathed them.

8. Ralph Fletcher Seymour, "Some Went This Way" (Ralph Fletcher Seymour, 1945) p.9.

9. Alson, Smith, "Chicago's Left Bank" (Regnery, 1953) p.167.

10. Hecht, "A Child of the Century" (Simon and Shuster, 1954) p.243.

Part III

From New Forms, New Freedoms

The Chicago evolution was so deep and so broad, and yet so abrupt that it changed America. A new spirit enlivened education, politics, racial attitudes, labor unions, social work, business and the law without many historians having noticed what had happened. Perhaps they missed the phenomenon because it was so simple: the people's lives had become more their own.

They Dared to Democratize Education

Two of the most radical, turn-of-the-century Chicagoans were Francis Parker and John Dewey. They earned that title not by throwing Marxist slogans into the air or furtively building bombs, but because they shared the deep belief that the beginning and the end of American education should be the common school and democracy.

Parker, principal of Chicago's teacher-training "Normal School" from 1883 until 1899, saw in crystalline terms the relationship between education and the democratic experience. He wrote:

> Democracy means the responsibility of all for each; the common school is the direct exposition of this fundamental principle; common education is the means to freedom.
>
> The children of today are in our hands; whatever we do for them will be the future. Our lack of faith in this direction is the greatest infidelity. To use a common illustration: A Kentucky farmer will look at a hundred colts and say, "I will train every one of them to become a useful horse." We look at the children and decide that we can save but a few of them; that many of them must become criminals, many of them a burden upon society; that many of them will enhance vice and put barriers in the way of our political institutions. We must believe we can save every child.

Parker's school was part of the Chicago public education system and was developed to be a leaven to test and spread these ideas throughout the Chicago schools.

Francis Parker, despite his contributions, is a little-known name. One of the facts which books on the history of education bother to recall about him is that he was a colonel in the Union army. The other is that he was a founder of progressive education in this country, having gone to Germany in 1872 to study the educational practices of Pestalozzi, Herbart and Froebel. He received better treatment in Adolph Meyer's "An Educational History of the American People" (Second edition, 1967) as well as in *Encyclopaedia Britannica* under both "Progressive Education" and his name. A quote from the latter expresses the thinking that best ought to be identified with his name:

> Parker emphasized arts and crafts and urged the correlation of subjects around a common core. Much of this was basically European, but Parker was no mere borrower. In an era when principals were tsars in their schools, he convened his teachers in weekly discussions and organized the first parent-teacher group in Chicago.

Also in Chicago a very similar approach would develop, which was to get far more attention, in John Dewey's famous "lab" school at the University of Chicago, or—as it was formally known—the University Elementary School.

Dewey was to pick up on much of the experience and many of the ideas of Francis Parker. The influence of these two would create progressive education.

John Dewey also had a strong and abiding "faith in Democracy as a guiding force in education." His ideas, were to upset many people and strikingly turn education around.

To understand where education was before Parker and Dewey, we can look to the study done for *Forum* magazine by Joseph Mayer Rice in 1892 and 1893. He was considered the first of the "muckrakers." He did his investigating well, interviewing 1,200 teachers from around the country for his articles, "The Public School System of the United States."

In his series, later published in a book, he spoke enthusiastically of Francis Parker's work in Chicago. Most of his attention, however, was devoted to American school system in its "absurdity."[1]

Speaking of New York primary schools, he wrote that the typical one:

> is a hard, unsympathetic, mechanical-drudgery school, a school into which the light of science has not yet entered. Its characteristic features lies in the severity of its discipline, a discipline of enforced silence, immobility, and mental passivity. The difference found in going from room to room and from school to school—I have seen many of them—are differences in degree only, and not in kind. One teacher will allow her pupils to move their heads a little more freely than the standard, another will allow a little more freedom to the shoulder joints but less freedom in moving the head, and a third teacher will require the students to keep their hands in their laps instead of behind their backs.[3]

"The aim of the teachers," he elaborates, "is simply to secure results by drilling the pupils in the facts prescribed for the grades."

"In order to reach the desired end," Rice laments, "the school has been converted into the most dehumanizing institution that I have ever laid eyes upon, each child being treated as if he possessed a memory and the faculty of speech, but no individuality, no sensibilities, no soul."

Many were aware of these great faults of the educational system, but it was Francis Parker and John Dewey, who, more than any others, did something about them. That their voices were coming out of Chicago was no accident. They both chose the lakeside metropolis in which to develop their reforms or, rather, systems of formation. Parker moved to Chicago in the 1880s after being superintendent of schools in Quincy, Massachusetts, for a short term. John Dewey's years devoted to education were synonymous with his teaching career in Chicago. His later ones were geared to philosophy and ethics rather than the technique and philosophy of education.

Former Harvard President James Conant pointed to the influence of Parker on the better-remembered Dewey:

> ...Parker and Dewey came to know each other, which had far reaching effects on American education. If one reads Col. Parkers' "Talks on Pedagogics" published in 1894 and John Dewey's "School and Society" published in 1899, the influence of the older

> man, with a rich teaching experienc, on the young philosopher is evident.[4]

In further comparing the two it is surprising to see the clarity and simplicity of Parker versus the abstract and academic writing of Dewey while both were homing in on the same question.

The irony in Chicago today is that there is a private school—an "alternate" school for affluent North Siders—that is named for Col. Francis Parker, the educator and democrat, who wrote the following words:

> The aristocratic idea of charity is still a potent influence in education. Our school system began as charity schools—charity schools such as the Volksschule of Germany. Many wealthy people who have the traditional or parvenu feeling of class distinction look today upon the common-school system as a charity and hold there should be one education for rich children and another for the poor; that the children of the rich should not mingle with and be contaminated by the children of the poor. I have had much to do with both classes, and I wish to say here that in my contact with the poorest children I have found as much of intrinsic morality and vigorous mental power in them as in rich children. This false idea of contamination is born of the past, a reappearance of the old-time aristocratic idea of separation and isolation...
>
> When, in American society, classes become permanent and the children in these classes are educated in separate schools, the doom of the republic is sealed. There can be no separated classes in a republic; the lifeblood of the republic must stream from the ground up; there can be no stratified society.[5]

In the school he supervised, Francis Parker translated his deep idealism into practical measures. No separation or isolation, to him, also meant no separation of the sexes from kindergarten on, an unheard-of idea in his day. It also meant elimination of the European system of education, where everything came down from the minister of education. In contrast, it has been said of Parker's pedagogy: "The essence of the new system was that there was no system about it; it was marked by intense individuality...Experiments were to be cautiously tried and results from time to time noted."

Joseph Rice noted in the New York schools he observed that the byword was "No one is responsible for anything. Whenever anything goes amiss, the power structure is so ordered that it is impossible to discover which one of the 165 officials is responsible."

Francis Parker wanted everyone responsible: administrators, educators, parents and the children. When evaluating education, he was willing to be specific as to where the greatest breakdown in that responsibility lay:

> The greatest barrier to making the common school what it can and should be is the profound indifference of the most intelligent people in regard to the possibilities of radical improvements.

Francis Parker could exist for almost 20 years in Chicago because it was a city that had room for such ideas. Even if many of the wealthy were opposed to them, they hadn't worked out the same class system and controls which older cities had.

It was to be John Dewey who projected that reform firmly into the national educational mainstream and met a seiche of opposition as never arose before or after in the history of American schools.

John Dewey's educational philosophy was born not only of his own "instrumental pragmatism" along with a good dose of Francis Parker, but also—according to his biographers—with a strong influence from the humanism of the University of Chicago and the deep humanitarianism of Jane Addams and Hull House.

His contemporaries at the University of Chicago included Thorstein Veblen, who wrote "The Theory of the Leisure Class," and other socio-political thinkers such as Edward Bemis, W. I. Thomas and Albion Small, who argued that "the conditions of life could be studied so as to reduce social failures."

Even more influential was his deep and warm relationship with Jane Addams of Hull House. He was on the settlement house's board of directors and took a very active part in its life, giving talks, conducting courses and entering regularly into discussions such as the midwinter Sunday afternoon Plato Club.

Jane Addams not only exuded a philosophy of equality and democracy, but also set a tone of being a practical fighter who knew how to get things done. Dewey did not take part in specific social crusades, but he learned from her social conscience and above all picked up a sense of how to go out from his ivy walls to fight practical battles in behalf of his philosophy.[6]

Dewey's educational approach—if it is fair so to simplify it—was as individual and child-centered as was Francis Parker's. Both believed a child's interest had to be a basic key to his or her education.

That concept was a tremendous emotional experience for teachers to confront. They were secure in the system in which John Dewey recalled being educated:

> School was a pretty deadly place when I attended. We were forced to learn a given number of pages of text and recite them orally the next day. The way we learned had no relation to the world we lived in. Discipline was then the key to education, a discipline inflicted with rawhide or a ruler. I remember how glad we were when vacation rolled around. We would sing: "Goodbye school, goodbye teacher, damned old fool!"[7]

Such rote education is still very much observable in schools across the country and throughout the world, but it is no longer the universal norm and accepted ideal since Francis Parker, John Dewey and progressive education entered the classroom picture.

The word among teachers who "knew someone" who had studied or taken a summer workshop at Dewey's University of Chicago lab school[8] was that he "lets children do whatever they want." Others said, "I'd like to see him do that with my hellions."

As one writer described Dewey's "non-system," however, "The children neither studied nor did what they pleased: but the idea was that if children had a sufficient variety of activities provided, they could be so arranged as to result in getting knowledge and in forming good habits of thought."[9]

Another very special side of Dewey's educational techniques was his use of materials such as wood, metal, leather, clay, etc. and the tools to work with them. The confusing phrase "manual training" was often used to describe what he was attempting. His meaning of it was far more basic and imaginative than the common, pedantic denotation of learning to use a lathe and a drill press.

For example, in the progressive classroom of John Dewey, the children were given the task of solving the problems of primitive man and retracing for themselves the steps in the industrial processes. They picked cotton, carded and spun it into cloth on machines of their own, which often they had designed.

Dewey's notion was to let the child repeat history rather than parroting a verbal version of it.

As an educator, he had paid attention equally to the importance of goals as well as techniques. An insight into his objectives and his own conscious awareness of man's social nature is seen in the statement by Dewey:

> We are apt to look at the school from an individualistic standpoint, as something between teacher and pupil, or between teacher and parent. That which interests us most is naturally the progress made by the individual child of our acquaintance, his normal physical development, his advance in ability to read, write, and figure, his growth in the knowledge of geography and history, improvement in manners, habits of promptness, order, and industry—it is from such standards as these that we judge the work of the school. And rightly so. Yet the range of the outlook needs to be enlarged. What the best and wisest parent wants for his own child, that must be the community want for all of its children. Any other ideal for our schools is narrow and unlovely; acted upon, it destroys our democracy. All that society has accomplished for itself is put, through the agency of the school, at the disposal of its future members. All its better thoughts of itself it hopes to realize through the new possibilities thus opened to its future self. Here individualism and socialism are at one. Only by being true to the full growth of all the individuals who make it up, can society by any chance be true to itself. And in the self-

> direction thus given, nothing counts as much as the school, for, as Horace Mann said, "Where anything is growing, one former is worth a thousand re-formers."[10]

To Dewey, the social grouping of children was to teach cooperative living. It was both an ideal and a technique for developing human intelligence.

The idea at times was carried to extremes, as were most of Dewey's new theories. Some teachers paralleled the child's development with European culture, letting him or her pass through several early stages of semi-savagery, then making them pagans and later teaching them the ideals of chivalry. They could get bad grades if they became "Christians" too soon.

Educators protested against Dewey and Parker's hypotheses, hesitating to "experiment with children," refusing to believe how poorly the status quo was working as an educational system. Mostly, however, they objected to the questioning and challenging of discipline as "the key to education," a point on which they could quote the educational philosophy of the Bible about sparing the rod and spoiling the child.

Even today it is not unusual to read an article in which some writer traces the "age of permissiveness" back to John Dewey. Professor James Conant looked at the charge scientifically rather than giving it the broadside many progressive educators would like to.

Conant wrote:

> Dewey and later his followers who were professors of education, added several elements of importance to the new pedagogic approaches of the 1890s and early 1900s. Indeed by 1919, when the Progressive Education Association was founded, the movement had acquired much ideological baggage, some of it related to psychology, some to sociology, and not a little to politics as well. It was to be an awkward load to carry and by no means as closely related to the basic principles as was at first maintained.
>
> Indeed, since the new pedagogic approach was early accepted in the elementary schools, it would be my contention that the permanent influence of the movement is to be found by examining what actually

> goes on in the classroom and not what the professors of education have had to say about it. In other words, it is important to separate the new techniques of teaching from some of the wider aims of the progressive movement, particularly those which were manifest in the Depression years.[11]

Today, Francis Parker's pure sense of democracy in education, and the child development techniques of John Dewey by Conant's standards seem more hopes and ideals than reality in America's schools.

1. Francis Parker's comments are drawn from a very strong piece he wrote in 1894 on "Democracy and the Common School." It appeared in a book he published that year titled "Talks on Pedagogics." Apparently, he was a little closer to the American language in choosing a title for a lesser known book he wrote. He called it "Talks on Teaching." The full text of his comments on democracy and schools is reprinted in "The Annals of America" (1976) Vol. II, p.575. There is also a 1937 reprint of "Talks on Pedagogics."

2. Joseph Mayer Rice's articles were reprinted in a book, "The Public School System of the United States" (1893) that has become the classic, methodical evaluation of the educational system against which other critiques are measured. The strong urge of a person reading the study is to want to see it duplicated today.

3. "The Annals of America," Vol. II, p.396.

4. Dr. James Conant wrote these comments in "Slums and Suburbs" (McGraw-Hill, 1961).

5. "Annals," p.579. Francis Parker School was started in 1901 by him not as an alternate school, but as a lab school, part of his work in training teachers after he had resigned as head of Normal School, where he had trained a generation of Chicago teachers. It was founded in connection with the University of Chicago, where he served with Dewey for a very short time before his death. There is also a Francis Parker public high school.

6. The relationship between John Dewey, his wife and Jane Addams was quite close, according to George Dykhuizen in "The Life and Mind of John Dewey" (Southern Illinois University Press, 1973) p.104-5. The Deweys named their daughter Jane after Miss Addams. Even more significantly, the author credited Jane Addams with confirming Dewey's "faith in Democracy as a ruling force in education." On the other hand, one cannot help but wish that John Dewey had given his manuscript of "Democracy and Education" (Macmillan Co., 1916) to Jane Addams before publication and she would have told him, "It's not empirical enough. Come on down to earth."

7. These Deweyan comments on education are from the Associated Press biographical sketch (issued 1930) on him. These short "bios" are regularly updated on all famous people so that in the event of the death (canonization, imprisonment or election as President), the newspapers would have them on hand.

8. Clashes with the Board of Education in 1899 led to Parker resigning his position at Normal and beginning his affiliation with the University of Chicago. Upon his death in 1902, John Dewey assumed the leadership of both his and Parker's schools, both associated with the university. Conflicts arising from that dual role led to Dewey leaving the university in 1904 and to a great extent removing himself from education and returning to the broader scope of

philosophy. Thus, both men were removed from situations in which they could have an effect on the introduction of the democratic process into the public school system (except through their writers and followers).

9. A good synopsis of John Dewey's teachings (and it's difficult to find a short, clear one) can be found in "Six Major Prophets" (Little Brown and Co., 1917) by Edwin Slosson. In many ways, World War I killed the whole idea of "Progressivism" and many movements that had used the word as a banner. The reason was that the progressive argued integrally that the world was getting better and that man was evolving more humanely every day. The suffering, brutality and wholesale slaughter of World War I was disillusioning to the point of destroying such optimistic reasoning.

10. "The School and Society," reprinted "John Dewey on Education," p.295 (Modern Library, 1964).

11. "Slums and Suburbs" (1961) p.139. It is well to note that the context of these comments are a comparison throughout the book of education needs, hopes and possibilities in the slums and in the suburbs.

Miss Jane Addams, democrat

Of all the invigorating breezes originating in Chicago and blowing across the nation at the turn-of-the-century, one of the freshest and strongest was Jane Addams, co-founder of Hull House.

Miss Addams' accomplishments are often jotted down like a laundry list that begins with her starting the world-famous Hull House in 1889 at Halsted and Polk streets and ending with her Nobel Peace Prize in 1931. Somehow, in this enumeration, Jane Addams gets lost in what she did. Her energy receives more emphasis than her purpose in expending it.

Simply put, Jane Addams of Chicago was one of the most deeply democratic people ever to have an influence on this nation. Others were strong in their fields—education, labor, politics, social welfare, suffrage, civil rights or peace—but she had a profound impact on America in every one of these areas through her work, her life, her speeches, her writing, her fame and her suffering.

She was a democrat in all things. Her nephew and biographer, James Linn, wrote of her:

> Here was a new voice in the American chorus, striking with precision and color a higher note than had been reached before.
>
> The essence of her message, purport of her intentions...was the necessity for progress in a democracy, the achievement of a life which shall be both good and common. Jane Addams went to Hull House to live, no more to help than to be helped; no more to provide opportunities for others than to be provided with an opportunity; no more to satisfy the longings of

> others than to satisfy her own longing; no more to "save" than to be "saved."[1]

Jane Addams had the democratic vision. Others who were working on part of it—Louis Sullivan, Eugene Debs, John Dewey, Julia Lathrop, Dr. Alice Hamilton, Upton Sinclair, Lyman Gage, Graham Taylor, Carl Sandburg—came to her for support, insight and rekindling.

Before her time, Americans gave lip service to democracy in politics and to the rights and dignity of people. They didn't even envision it, however, in such of the nation's institutions as schools, factories, art, architecture, newspapers, families, literature, charities and economics. The national ideal was to become a self-made millionaire and then to flower as a philanthropist.

Jane Addams excoriated the philanthropists mercilessly because they represented the opposite of democracy.

In 1907, she wrote:

> The successful businessman who is also a philanthropist is in more than the usual danger of getting widely separated from his employees. The men already have the American veneration for wealth and successful business capacity, and added to this, they are dazzled by his good works. The workmen have the same kindly impulses as he, but while they organize their charity into mutual benefit associations and distribute their money in small amounts in relief for widows and insurance for the injured, the employer may build model towns, erect college buildings, which are tangible and enduring, and thereby display his goodness in concentrated form.[2]

It was a theme she would often repeat. On another occasion, she restated it thus:

> In so far as philanthropists...are cut off from the great moral life springing from our common experiences, so long as they are "good people" rather than "with them," they are bound to accomplish a large amount of harm.[3]

Because she was open to the goodness of other people, even the most "brutish," she was exhilarated. She said of it:

> As the acceptance of democracy brings a certain life-giving power, so it has its own sanctions and comforts. Perhaps the most obvious one is the curious sense which comes to us from time to time that we belong to the whole, that a certain basic well being can never be taken away from us whatever the turn of fortune.

Jane Addams' sense of democracy was not something she gained from theorizing or studying. It came to her from her experiences and was constantly renewed by those experiences, a point that she made time and again.

And while Chicago was fortunate to have Jane Addams as its most illustrious citizen, she was blessed to have the city, for it was the source of most of her experiences, relationships and opportunities.

The Chicago democrats such as Eugene Debs (during his period here), Louis Sullivan, John Dewey and John Peter Altgeld who came to her perspective also gave her insight.[4] She was open to them when they were unpopular and drank deep from the experience.

A group from which she learned even more was the women of Hull House, strong personages whose lives intertwined with hers. Each scored major victories for the people of Chicago on their own.

Ellen Gates Starr founded Hull House with Jane Addams. She was open immediately to Jane Addams' idea of committing themselves to the idea of starting it. She was a sensitive and enthusiastic teacher, a good one who organized art classes and reading clubs at Hull House and in the community.

Julia Lathrop, also a resident and a person about whom Jane Addams was to write a book, did much to make sociology and social work professions. She was a strong influence in the very thorough study of the Hull House neighborhood that took the neighborhood block by block, highlighting the needs and problems of each. The book even classifies brothels according to price. It was a major step in making sociology a science that can ferret out a community's needs rather than simply deal with those that surface by themselves.[5]

Florence Kelley, yet another very active resident, was made chief factory inspector of the State of Illinois in 1895 by Governor Altgeld. She was also to become for 30 years the executive head of the National Consumers' League.

While Florence Kelley fought in the public arena and later in the courts for better factory conditions and against the miserable sweatshop conditions that existed in the Hull House area, another person who was part of Hull House made an even more lasting contribution in industrial safety. She was Dr. Alice Hamilton. Her specialty became occupational diseases and industrial poisoning. She was eventually to "graduate" to Washington to work for the federal government and finally to serve as professor of industrial medicine at Harvard.

All of them were strong personalities, articulate and dedicated. They shared in Jane Addams's vision, but they also contributed to it, making Hull House and Jane Addams deeply feminine and strong in her belief in women's suffrage.

Her views were also greatly influenced by the people in her neighborhood, who found her home an open house. She once cited, for example, an error in sensitivity she and her fellow residents made toward the community in their first year. It was about the burial of a little child who had died after being abandoned. The Hull House women questioned the desire of neighbors to chip in for a funeral as being a little too late to help. She wrote of the incident years later:

> It is doubtful if Hull-House has ever done anything which injured it so deeply in the minds of its neighbors. It was only forgiven by the most indulgent on the ground that the residents were spinsters, and could not know a mother's heart. No one born and reared in the community could possibly have made a mistake like that. No one who had studied the ethical standards with any care could have bungled so completely.[6]

As her experiences and sharing with the community increased, it became very simple for Jane Addams and her co-workers to avoid such pitfalls. Their goal was not to be as "good as they could be" toward the poor, but to share in the simple everyday kindness of people toward each other.

She loved to contrast the benevolence of the ward bosses with the guarded generosity of various organizations and people who wanted to be "good" to the poor. The saloon politicians often came out looking better in her comments despite the dedicated battles she waged against them in the community. Speaking of one such political boss, she wrote:

> He distributes each Christmas many tons of turkeys not only to voters, but to families who are represented by no vote. By a judicious management some families get three or four turkeys apiece; but, what of that, the alderman has none of the nagging rules of the charitable societies, nor does he declare that because a man wants two turkeys for Christmas, he is a scoundrel who should never be allowed to eat turkey again.[7]

Her writings are full of such experiences she learned from living in Chicago. She was constantly in the middle of what was happening not only in the neighborhood, but also in the city.

Hull House at Polk and Halsted streets was to acquire 13 buildings. There were a handful of settlement houses in the world before it. In particular, Toynbee Hall in London is credited with being the first. William T. Stead of England, who by 1893 visited all of them, pronounced Hull House the "best because it is the most helpful." He attributed Hull House's superiority as being "perhaps due to the fact that a woman, with a woman's instinct for motherliness is the head of Hull House whereas the other institutions are all more or less under the supervision of men."[8]

By then Hull House had a day-care center, college extension courses, a branch of the Public Library, a public bath, concerts, a gymnasium, a women's club, a co-operative coal yard, a coffee house, debating society, science clubs and any number of community action programs.

People came from the world around to talk with and meet Jane Addams. Her name was synonymous with the good forces and ideas radiating out of Chicago.

In 1894, she became so deeply involved in Eugene Debs' struggle with Pullman that the union's defeat crushed her. She, however, helped lift up the defeated organizers after the battle and spoke often and loud of them as heroes.

She actually accepted a job with the city...as garbage inspector for the Nineteenth Ward. She rode herd over the city garbage collectors and private firms, often taking them into court and, in one case, finding pavement under eight inches of trash.

She was very close to educator John Dewey and even more democratic in her concept of learning than he. She wanted his innovations quickly for every student. Addressing herself to the hopes of education, she wrote:

> As democracy modifies our concept of life, it constantly raises the value and function of each member of the community, however humble he may be. We have come to believe that the most "brutish man" has a value in our common life, a function to perform which can be fulfilled by no one else. We are gradually requiring of the educator that he shall free the powers of each man and connect with the rest of life. We ask this not merely because it is the man's right to be thus connected, but because we have become convinced that the social order cannot afford to get along without his special contribution.[9]

In the 1890s, Jane Addams shared her beliefs in democracy through the frequent discussion groups and meetings both informal and organized at Hull House and through lectures throughout the city. In the next decade her lectures increasingly were across the country and she wrote, during these years, three major books: "Democracy and Social Ethics," "The Spirit of Youth and the City Streets" and "Twenty Years at Hull House."

Despite the tremendous tolerance in her personality, the list of people who considered her the enemy began to grow. She publicly championed unpopular men such as Altgeld, Debs and Dewey. She visited an anarchist in jail immediately after President McKinley was assassinated (by a man who proclaimed himself to be an anarchist).[10] More than anything, however, people were coming to realize that her words about democracy were not pious platitudes, but plans of action. Ultimately, democracy means a sharing of decision-making and of power. Those who arbitrarily held power in politics, in business, in the press, as male voters, in the military, in education and even in religion could be charmed only so much by a person who stood opposed to that distribution of power.

Still, it was not until the United States' entry into World War I that her enemies were to watch Jane Addams fall from the esteem of being the most admired woman in the nation. In 1916, she came out in behalf of presidential candidate Woodrow Wilson because she felt he was genuinely committed to keeping the United States out of the war.

Wilson was ecstatic over her endorsement. The papers claimed it meant 1,000,000 votes among women, who were finally getting the right of the ballot in many states and who saw Jane Addams as their leader. In 1915, she had journeyed to the Hague, the Netherlands, to preside over a meeting of women from warring and neutral nations. The group later organized as the Women's International League for Peace and Freedom, of which Jane Addams would be president until her death.

But just as with Debs, Altgeld, Sullivan, Parker and other turn-of-the-century Chicagoans who offered their nation belief in democracy, Jane Addams was marked to suffer. The attacks—personal and venomous, in print and in letters—flooded into Jane Addams as the United States government began to psyche its people to be willing to kill Germans. Pacifists became equated with traitors and Jane Addams was the most visible target of all. Worse, her goals of peace were deeply frustrated and the man whom she had helped put in the White House led the nation into war.

Ever the person who believed in "you do what you can," Jane Addams geared her effort away from the seemingly impossible in terms of a voluntary peaceful retrenchment and toward forcing the various sides to agree to humane treatment of prisoners and the protection of non-combatants.

She died of cancer on May 21, 1935. Despite the fact that she slowly regained her stature among the people in the 16 years after the war and even though she shared the Nobel Peace Prize in 1931, her later years did not have the zest of her earlier ones. She had been worn out by battles and by bad health. Her associates had constantly watched her push herself when she was dead tired. But the wear and tear did not bring discouragement great enough to force her to give up her belief in democracy and its manifold experiences.

She never married, but she did get to know "a mother's heart," because she gave Chicago one of its most legitimate children, Hull House.

1. "Jane Addams: A Biography," (D. Appleton-Century, 1935) p.106. Her two autobiographical books "Twenty years at Hull House" (The Macmillan Co., 1911) and "Second Twenty Years at Hull House" (The Macmillan Co., 1930) lack the zest and drive of some of her other writings. Certainly, one of the better books about her is the one we quote here. Another published that same year is "Jane Addams of Hull House" by W. E. Wise (Harcourt, Brace & Co., 1935).

2. The comment is from "Democracy and Social Ethics" (The Macmillan Co., 1907) p.153. The work is unquestionably her most optimistic look at democracy and contains many of her most eloquent statements. In it, she is arguing in behalf of a practical ethic that includes charity and charitable works but not self-serving philanthropy. The latter had become very popular among the new millionaires of Chicago. In her "Second Twenty Years at Hull House" written in 1930 and after seeing multiple rejections of her ideas, she had allowed some disallusionment to creep into her views.

3. This quotation is from the excellent overview of this period by Ray Ginger, "Altgeld's America" (Funk & Wagnalls, 1958) p.143. No source is given for the quote and it is very similar to comments from "Democracy and Social Ethics." It is more succinct in Ginger's book, so either Jane Addams said it better at a different time or else someone took liberties and made it snappier.

4. Jane Addams and Clarence Darrow, however, were at odds. He was a cynic; she, an optimist. He was avowedly against the system, while she tried to make the most of it. He was closer to the law and she was probably closer to the people. According to his biographer Irving Stone in "Clarence Darrow for the Defense" (Doubleday, Doran and Company, 1941) p.115, he felt Hull House accepted too much from philanthropic sources instead of relying on self-help organizations. They each represent a divergence of theory in solving the problems of humanity.

5. The Macmillan Company published several Hull House books during this era that contributed much to modern sociology. Jane Addams wrote: "The Spirit of Youth and the City Streets" (1910) and "A New Conscience and an Ancient Evil" (1912). The very thorough study of the area is contained in "Hull House Maps and Papers" (1895), simply "by the Residents of Hull House." Florence Kelley wrote "The Working Child" in 1896 and Julia Lathrop published, through the Illinois Federation of Women's Clubs in 1905, a book with the very blunt title, "Suggestions for Visitors to the County Poorhouses and Other Public Charitable Institutions." This little volume represents well the tone of Hull House. It's not a be-on-your-best-behavior book, but an effort to turn visitors into investigators and ultimately into reformers. Addams, Lathrop and the other women of Hull House were deliberately and meanly denied credit for the early works in sociology, according to Mary Jo Deegan in her 1988 book "Jane

Addams and the Men of the Chicago School:1892-1918" (Transaction Books, Rutgers, 1988.)

6. "Democracy and Social Ethics" (Macmillian, 1902) p.242.

7. "Democracy and Social Ethics" p.243. It is interesting to note in light of these comments that this was the same time as Lincoln Steffens wrote "The Shame of the Cities" (1904).

8. "If Christ Came to Chicago," (Laird and Lee, 1894) p.412. The climaxing vision of Stead's book however, is the final chapter titled "In the Twentieth Century." In it, he optimistically sees Hull House affiliates in every one of the (city's) two thousand precincts, who were living among the people, sharing their life and constantly interchanging their experience for the purpose of bringing the help of all to those in need" p.428.

9. This quote (p.178) forms the opening of her chapter, "Educational Methods," in "Democracy and Social Ethics." It is surprising that the chapter is not more specifically involved in the new educational system being pioneered by her friend, John Dewey. It does, however, parallel his criticism of the then current state of education.

10. Cornelia Meggs in her book "Jane Addams: Pioneer for Social Justice" (Little, Brown and Company, 1970) on p. 160 elaborates on this visit as the turning-off point in Jane Addams' public veneration.

Grover Cleveland Sends Troops to Occupy Chicago

Chicago was the scene of a massive labor struggle between two men, with the loser going to jail and the winner's body having to be buried in yards of concrete so his "ungrateful" employees could not retaliate after his death.

The year was 1894 and the contestants were union leader Eugene V. Debs and sleeping car magnate George M. Pullman.

The issue was industrial democracy, the right of workers to unionize.

Chicago in the main sympathized with and supported Debs and the strikers. President Grover Cleveland sided with Pullman's interests and sent federal troops to occupy the city of Chicago, to move the mail trains and to break the strike.

Cleveland and Pullman won. The workers and Chicago lost. But the city had learned a precious lesson about rights, freedom and democracy.

The struggle would prove a turning point in Chicago's direction and ultimately, in the nation's history...most especially because it would be another 40 years before unskilled workers would be successful in their efforts to form or join non-craft unions.

Pullman's roots in Chicago had gone back to the 1850s, when his ingenuity had helped literally raise the city out of the mud, by having hundreds of men simultaneously turn large handscrews to lift supports beneath major buildings such as the Tremont House hotel.[1]

In the early 1860s, George Pullman had devised an ingenious sleeping car for railroad passengers, using principles which were to last 100 years in the construction of such coaches. Adeptly employing his car to bear Lincoln's body in the 1865 funeral train, he received national attention and was able to convince the various railroads to adjust their different tracks gauges to accommodate his luxury item.

He drove a hard bargain with the railroads because he knew he had an exclusive product. With this, and high-pressure sales techniques, Pullman squeezed out competitors. In 1890, U.S. Senator John Sherman, author of the Sherman Anti-Trust Law; nevertheless, wanted the government to investigate why Pullman accommodations cost passengers so much and still were far from satisfactory. He called the Pullman Company one of the worst two monopolies in the United States.2

Some historians credit Pullman at least with good intentions in building his company town of Pullman, on the south edge of Chicago. In doing so, they describe the beauty of a 3,500 acre workingman's "paradise," the paternalistic "good nature" of the man and even the solicitude of his wife.3

George Pullman built HIS model town to order and to control his employees' lives. He had the noted architect S.S. Beman design it in 1879, claiming facetiously that it was named after the first syllable of his own name and the last syllable of Beman's.

It was definitely a for-profit venture. Pullman made money even off the water and gas he purchased and sold to his employees.4

Tourists came from around the world to admire Pullman's great accomplishment and "act of kindness."

In 1882, however, his lack of benevolence became apparent. One thousand who were not yet moved into the town under construction struck Pullman over the question of a travel allowance he had arbitrarily cut off. Not one of them ever worked for the company again.

None of the facilities in Pullman—which included an opera house, a library and a number of churches—were free. One of the churches stood vacant for a long time because no one could pay the high rent the Pullman Company demanded.

The model town's housing units were quite good for its day, but the rents were also high. The city, however, being built from scratch, still managed to have its own slum for those employees even poorer than the rest.5

In 1885, Pullman trounced the Knights of Labor in an attempted strike. His intransigence over the next eight years made him a symbol of everything the labor movement stood against.

In 1893, at the tail end of the World's Columbian Exposition, the nation and the city were hit by one of the most severe Depressions in the country's history.

Pullman, who controlled the water rates, the rent and gas prices in his town, refused to lower them as he sliced wages by one-third and cut employment severely. The residents were furious and some of them desperate. Pullman did not allow them to get behind in their bills, but they couldn't afford to move and were too poor to survive on Pullman's terms.

Nationally, there was only one union winning any strikes and only one man organizing the unorganized. He was Eugene V. Debs, who had come out of the Brotherhood of Locomotive Firemen to start a new, catch-all American Railway Union.6 His efforts were not 100 percent endorsed by the traditional unions, which were organized on a craft basis even in the railroad industry and which had virtually given up trying to strike no matter how bad the conditions or wages.

Debs himself had the reputation of being a very dedicated man, but also had proved a moderate in the use of strikes.

Pullman employees joined his newly-formed and fast-growing labor union. Their eligibility for membership in the American Railway Union was not predicated on the basis that they manufactured cars for railroads but on the technical grounds that there were several miles of track in the plant and on the grounds.7

Conditions were so bad that a meeting of employees voted unanimously to strike, despite caution warnings from American Railway Union president Debs who, at the time, was home in Terre Haute, Indiana. Three thousand workers walked off the job May 11, 1894 and the company quickly laid off the remaining 300. The strikers posted guards around the plant to make certain no damage would be done to company property. The desperation of the strikers was evident in a statement by their chairman, Thomas Heathcote:

> We do not expect the company to concede to our demands. We do not know what the outcome will be, and in fact we do not much care. We do know that we are working for less wages than will maintain ourselves and families in the necessities of life, and on that proposition we absolutely refuse to work any longer.

An example of what he was talking about was furnished by a skilled mechanic who worked 10 hours a day for 12 days and then received a paycheck for 7 cents. It had been for $9.07, but $9 rent for the company-owned house was deducted ahead of time.

Debs was not optimistic about the outcome, but he had talent for handling strike situations and knew how to bring every non-violent tactic to bear. And peaceful he wanted to keep it, because the press and companies in such situations were as quick to seize upon an incident of violence as Hitler would later prove in attempting to justify his military conquests of neutral countries.

In June, Debs' union held its national convention in Chicago and discussed the possibility of a national boycott by the 125,000 members against handling Pullman cars or any train pulling them in the country, The argument was to pressure the Pullman company as it was paid a royalty or mileage allowance as the cars were used.[8]

The labor leader's reluctance continued, as he counseled against a precipitous boycott. He worried that there were too many unemployed railroad workers in the country who could be used to break the back of the union. The pleas of Pullman employees, however, prevailed, especially that of a young woman who told the convention how she had to pay back to the company out of her checks a debt of $70 owed by her deceased father. It amounted to over two months wages for her.

The boycott began on June 26 and grew around the country for almost a week without a major incident. Many of the newspapers, horrified at the power of the unions, launched personal attacks on Debs, with the *Chicago Tribune* editorial writers claiming he was a dictator, while protesting that no one had the working man's interest more at heart than they themselves did. The *New York Times* was worse. It found a doctor who claimed the labor leader once had been treated for dipsomania and the paper inferred that Debs was therefore incompetent.[9]

Debs played all of his cards well and should have won the game. For example, he personally kept in touch with all the strike chairmen throughout the country and stayed on top of any possibility of violence, preaching against it in every way and at each opportunity he could.

He didn't hold all the right cards, however, and he found himself trumped by non-support from craft union pioneer Samuel Gompers and the American Federation of Labor, who couldn't put their hearts into a strike by non-craft workers.

The other trump laid upon him was the actions of the United States Attorney General Richard Olney, a former corporation lawyer who had mainly represented railroads.

Olney argued that the strike was illegal and that the federal government had every right to use all possible means to end it. These included getting a sweeping injunction against the labor leaders forbidding them to answer questions, send telegrams or in any way aid the boycott.

Secondly, Olney convinced President Grover Cleveland to send federal troops into Chicago to maintain order and to keep mail trains moving. His action was illegal and belligerent in light of the fact that the mayor of Chicago and the governor of Illinois specifically told the President the troops were unnecessary and could not come into a state unless requested by the governor or unless they were in open rebellion.10

The governor, John Peter Altgeld, was one of Debs' best cards. He had used state militia to quell local outbreaks of violence, something Debs did not object to. Debs did, however, dread the federal troops and the thousands of deputy federal marshalls being recruited across the country. His fears were justified as clashes between the two federal groups and local crowds resulted in 13 deaths. Debs was able to claim with pride that not one member of his union was involved in any of these clashes.

In order to deal with the injunction, Debs sought out the best legal mind he could find. The man he chose was fairly young and, it turned out, in the employ of the Chicago and North Western Railroad as legal counsel. He was Clarence Darrow, destined to be the greatest lawyer any underdog would ever have. Darrow at first hesitated, but then had no trouble in quitting his job and going to work for the union.

Debs and other union leaders were cited with contempt of court by the judge who issued the injunction and indicted for conspiracy to obstruct a mail train on the Rock Island Railroad.

The timidity of the American Federation of Labor, the tremendous power of the federal government, the violence that arrived with the soldiers and the imprisonment of Debs combined and broke the strike.11 Pullman conceded nothing. Striking workers were not hired back.

The *Chicago Tribune* on July 15 patted itself on the back:

> The *Tribune* repeatedly warned them [the strikers] that such [the collapse of the strike] would be the inevitable outcome of their short-sighted action and for this is was roundly denounced by the salaried agitators, some of whom were asses enough to propose

> that it [the *Tribune*] be included in a comprehensive boycott of institutions and individuals which they supposed to be unfriendly to them and their cause. In reality, the Tribune was the truest and best friend of the deluded strikers and showed its friendship by trying to induce them to look at the matter in a sensible, practical light and thereby keep out of the pit.

The defeat was not one merely for the union. The people of Chicago had supported the strike, as had workers elsewhere. Mayor John Hopkins, who owned a large grocery store, contributed 25,000 pounds of flour and meat to a relief fund for those in need. The Chicago labor movement demanded action from Gompers and thousands quit work in sympathy for the strike.

Newspaper boys wore the white ribbon adopted by the strikers and often threw bundles of papers unsympathetic to the strike into sewers.

The defeat was a resounding one for Debs and the labor movement. Unions for the non-skilled were knocked out of the picture until the 1930s, when the law and the climate changed. Until then, in every situation the railroads and their detectives had the upper hand over any non-skilled or yard worker who tried for something better.

Darrow had little trouble making a shambles of the government's case against Debs and fellow union leaders. A juror took sick, however, and a mistrial was declared and no further effort was made to prosecute the case. Informal polls of the jury had it leaning 11 to 1 in favor of acquittal.

The great jury lawyer, however, was not able to convince the Supreme Court that a judge could not simply sentence people to jail without a trial or hearings on contempt charges. The issue would arise again over 70 years later in Chicago during the Conspiracy 7 trial and the court would rule otherwise.

Debs and his associates consequently served out three- and six-month contempt sentences in the Woodstock jail, which were only cells in the home of the McHenry County sheriff. They were shown almost unlimited freedom and pleasantness.

Pullman, on the other hand, was trapped in his own bitterness and a feeling he had been treated ungratefully by the employees for whom he felt he had done so much. His victory was to prove shallow despite the statement he issued:

> The public should not permit the real question which has been before it to be obscured. That question was as to the possibility of the creation and duration of a dictatorship which could make all the industries of the United States and the daily comfort of the millions dependent upon them, hostages for the granting of the fantastic whim of such a dictator. Any submission to him [Debs] would have been a long step in that direction, and in the interest of every law-abiding citizen of the United States was not to be considered for a moment.[12]

The strain of the fight and what Pullman accounted ingratitude is said to have contributed to his failing health and his death in 1897, three years after the strike. The town of Pullman, which had earlier been incorporated into Chicago by a vote of residents, had proved a deep disappointment, especially when the Illinois Supreme Court took away his own "fantastic whim" by forcing the company to give up all municipal functions in Pullman.

Pullman was buried along with the richest of Chicago millionaires in Graceland Cemetery near his fellow club members, Potter Palmer and Marshall Field. Beneath the surface, however, his grave is far different from theirs as yards and yards of cement and special casings were used to protect him even in death from his "ungrateful" former employees.[13]

George Pullman, however, had badly misjudged the situation and could have saved his heirs the expense. Chicago workers felt that much of his feudalism was buried with him and they were glad to see it stay there.[14]

1. Chicago in the 1850s was less than 20 years old, and was finding a severe limitation the swamp upon which the city had been built. Pullman's efforts, therefore, were both timely and critical to its future growth. According to Lewis and Smith in "Chicago: The History of Its Reputation" (Harcourt, Brace and Company, 1929), it took 1,200 men and 5,000 jackscrews to raise the hotel. On the signal, each man gave four jackscrews a turn to raise it half an inch.

2. The other was the Sugar Trust. Rev. William Carwardine in "The Pullman Strike" (Charles H. Kerr Co. 1973 edition) p.62 quotes Senator Sherman at length.

3. William Stead—who was not entirely in sympathy with the strikers—had the harshest words for Pullman. In "If Christ Came to Chicago" (Laird & Lee, 1894) p.87, Stead wrote: "The autocrat of all the Russias could not more absolutely disbelieve in government by the people, for the people, through the people, than George Pullman (did)." Stead (p.86) tells us that the town of Pullman was actually modeled after the Krupp (cannon manufacturers) family's venture in Essen, Germany.

4. The actual price Pullman paid for gas was 33 cents per thousand cubic feet, according to Stead. What the sleeping car magnate then charged his employees was $2.25 per thousand cubic feet.

5. The built-to-order slum in Pullman was known as "the brick yards," Rev. William H. Carwardine reported. The author was a Protestant pastor in the town of Pullman at the time of the strike. His "The Pullman Strike", was republished by Charles Kerr & Co. He describes "the brick yards" as four rows of shanties that could have been built for $100 each, but which rented for $96 annually (p.23).

6. Debs, a few months before, had garnered a spectacular victory for his union against James J. Hill's Great Northern railroad complex. Hill had ordered anyone even sympathetic to the union fired, but Debs had won both recognition and the restoration of a pay cut. That victory, according to Ray Ginger, lined up the sides for the Pullman strike battle. Samuel Gompers of the American Federation of Labor—an old friend of Debs—refused to accredit the fledgling non-craft union.

7. President Grover Cleveland in his 1904 self-justification lecture at Princeton University used the point of no direct connection between the Pullman employees and the railroads to attempt to establish his case. He called his talk, "The Government in the Chicago Strike of 1894," ignoring the name most used, "The Pullman Strike." His title was repeated when it was published in book form (Princeton University, 1913).

8. Pullman's "cold and arrogant language" ultimatum, according to Carwardine (p.29), was: "Nothing to arbitrate."

9. Ray Ginger elaborates on the *New York Times'* "yellow journalism" in

this matter in his biography of Debs, "The Bending Cross" (p.145). For the *Chicago Tribune's* fear of Debs as the worst of all menaces, see Philip Kinsley's "*The Chicago Tribune*: Its First Hundred Years" (*Chicago Tribune*, 1946) Vol. III p.247.

10 . Cleveland in his lecture (p.44-5) called Altgeld's arguments "dreary" and wound up the exchange curtly by stating "discussion may well give way to active efforts on the part of all in authority to restore obedience to law and to protect life and property."

11 . Various sources cite different points at which the strike failed, or rather the opposition to it succeeded. Cleveland, of course, felt his injunction and sending of troops "brought about a termination of the difficulty," Debs specifically pointed to the actions (and inactions) of the craft railroad unions and others claimed it was Gompers' "rigid neutrality" particularly at the crucial last minute.

12 . Ray Ginger, "The Bending Cross" (Rutgers, 1949) p.150.

13 . Emmett Dedmon in "Fabulous Chicago" (Random House, 1953) p.245 gives a graphic description of the lead-lined coffin, room-sized subterranean vault, asphalt, enforced steels rails and layers of concrete used in the two-day burial ceremony.

14 . The historic, national implications of the strike were not introduced by Pullman himself, analyst Colston E. Warne points out in "The Pullman Boycott of 1894: The Problem of Federal Intervention" (D.C. Heath and Co., 1955). Pullman was a local tyrant, not very different from company town owners in other industries at the time. They, too, were involved at one time or other in bloody strikes. The Pullman strike or boycott was far different because of Grover Cleveland's intervention and the broad use of the injunction; but even more important because those were used against what had good hopes of being a successful effort on the part of non-skilled workers to unionize. The era was a Depression one, with conditions not dissimilar to those in the 1930s, when the Congress of Industrial Unions (CIO) would be formed and factory workers organized. Providing a thorough background and bibliography on the Pullman strike, Warne's booklet is composed of "selected readings" on it.

The Chicago Platform Turns the Democratic Party Around

In Chicago, a new wave of leadership wrested control of the Democratic Party from East Coast domination.

The year was 1896.

Some say William Jennings Bryan did it. A closer scrutiny shows that it was Chicagoan John Peter Altgeld.

Critics proclaimed he was handing the party over to populists and crackpots. Supporters bragged it was being given to the people, especially the immigrants, the farmers, the workers and the poor.

The Democratic Party, history now shows, then and there cut its ties with the incumbent administration of Democratic President Grover Cleveland and with the monopolies. It oriented itself toward the interests of poorer people and sowed the seeds of the programs which would flourish under the New Deal, the New Frontier and the Great Society.

The occasion was the 1896 Democratic National Convention held in the Coliseum on Chicago's South Side. It was an event made famous in history by Bryan's "Cross of Gold" speech.

In arguing that the strong hand was really Altgeld's, Ray Ginger writes:

> Altgeld's strategy was simple. He would win labor and reformers by a broad program of social reconstruction. He would use the silver issue to win farm areas and the silver-producing states of the West. With the support of these groups he would oust the Eastern conservatives from their own party, and the Democracy would once more stand proudly in the anti-monopoly tradition of Jefferson and Jackson.[1]

And he did it. In June, 1895, a special convention called by the Democratic Party of Illinois declared for the free coinage of silver. During the next year Altgeld diligently organized the free-silver forces throughout the Ohio Valley, and in 1896 he was chosen chairman of the Illinois delegation to the Democratic National Convention. When that convention met in July, he was the most influential man present. Plank after plank bore the mark of his thinking, and around this document, the Chicago Platform of 1896, would swirl the struggles for a full decade thereafter for control of the Democratic Party in Illinois and in the nation.[2]

The real struggle was between two men: John Peter Altgeld, Governor of Illinois, and Grover Cleveland, former Governor of New York. Cleveland was president of the United States and Altgeld almost certainly would have been at least the Democratic nominee had he not been barred by the Constitutional requirement of having to be born in the United States.

Cleveland represented not only the East, but business and economic conservatism. It is sometimes said that to his credit, he held to his principles even when they became extremely unpopular in the face of a three-year Depression.

Altgeld was a democrat, with a small "d." He represented Chicago, as Cleveland did the East. He was not only aware of the city's and the nation's swelling population of immigrants, but also was one. His sympathy was with the poor and the worker, and he had pioneered progressive legislation. He suffered, in return, ridicule and vituperation. Of him, it was said by his enemies that he would never be able to understand the American mind because he was not born here. He had a vision, however, and moved to change the American consensus in the direction of democracy and personal freedom.

In many ways, Altgeld and Cleveland were the most representative men the two wings of the Democratic party could put in the ring to fight it out once and for all. And, it was Chicago against New York. In actuality, they were both to serve as seconds in the 1896 election. Altgeld was to be represented by William Jennings Bryan and Cleveland by John M. Palmer, who would subsequently run independently as a "Gold Democrat." Neither would win the presidency but Altgeld by far got the better of the fight, for his cause outlived them all.[3]

President Cleveland's policies had been deeply offensive to Altgeld, who had enthusiastically campaigned throughout Chicago and Illinois for him four years before in 1892. Cleveland repeatedly refused to "interfere with business" despite the fact that monopolies held an octopus embrace on the economy. He had vetoed legislation that would have given the poor and the farmer help in a deflated economy. And the two had personally clashed over the Pullman Strike in Chicago in 1894.

In telegrams between them, Altgeld had pleaded that the President had no need and no right to send federal troops into Chicago to "move the mails" as Cleveland had said he did. The language of the correspondence showed much of the gulf between the men and what they represented.

Altgeld's words were about needs and men's rights. They were eloquent, if sometimes tortuously written. And, because justice was the issue, one finds the Illinois governor precise in his legal arguments. Mainly, however, they are pleas meant not to criticize the President but to move him.

Cleveland's telegrams were short and dogmatic. They had no fervor except the cold passion of righteousness.[4] The troops stayed. Firing at and killing a number of bystanders, they served the two-fold purpose of moving the mails and breaking the strike.

The Chicago Democratic National Convention of 1896 took up the record of Cleveland, who was not running for re-election. An amendment was offered that stated: "We commend the honesty, economy, courage and fidelity of the present Democratic National Administration." It was defeated 564 to 357. Cleveland was repudiated by his fellow Democrats.[5] The power of the party had shifted to the Middle West. It also had veered away from business and toward the worker.

Altgeld helped the party make the switch almost despite himself. He was not an attractive man and he had a nervous twitch. And he had more than his share of enemies.

Altgeld was actively disliked and hated by large segments of the American public, thanks to the image the press gave of him. Parents pointed out to their children what an evil man he was. They called him either a socialist because of his policies or an "anarchist" because he had pardoned the two men remaining in prison in the aftermath of the Haymarket trial.

The 1890s was an age when an active and militant hatred toward anyone born in a foreign country was fanned by resentment toward the waves of immigrants coming into the country with their different ways and customs and their poverty. Altgeld's parents had brought him to this country when he was three months old. Therefore he was a "foreigner."

On the other hand, Altgeld built his political base on his sense of democracy and social justice. A three year Depression across the country united the farmer, the worker and the immigrant by the bond of their poverty.

The issue that Altgeld rode had been on the national scene for years and he pushed a resolution of it. The problem was deflation.

In an age which has had only inflation, it is difficult today to understand that deflation can be a serious problem. But it was a crushing one in 1895-6. Money was scarce and had been for so long that it kept going up in value. That was good for those who had money, but not for people who had debts. Farmers, for example, who had their lands and machinery mortgaged or were paying for it on time discovered that they were being paid for their crops at deflated prices, but still had to pay their debts at full value.

Altgeld and others argued that the United States had to help solve the problem by putting more money into circulation, thus creating an inflation to counterbalance the deflation. In order to do this, the United States would have to start minting silver coins as well as gold coins on a large scale and would have to break with the international gold standard in printing bills. The latter action, which most of the world took in the 1930s, was a "radical" answer in 1896.

The poor—especially the farmers—understood what deflation and going off the gold standard could mean in 1896, even if President Cleveland didn't. As a result, there was no chance he could have run for a third term. He had no conception, however, that he and his economic policies would be so totally rejected at his party's convention.

The "Chicago Platform" was a repudiation of Cleveland's economics and, in their place, a specific program by which the country could counter deflation and the Depression.

At the convention, Altgeld didn't actually write the provisions of the platform, but in the months before it he had diligently and adamantly set them up. He was not to be a candidate to succeed himself as governor in 1896. Because he didn't have to fight that battle or promote himself personally, he was at an advantage in his campaign to prepare the direction of the upcoming convention. His opponents, seeing this, tried the ruse of booming his candidacy. He ignored it. Had he not, they would have been able to argue he was trying to get attention focused on his own campaign.

At a meeting on May 19, 1896, he publicly laid out his plan for economic and monetary reform. He proposed that silver be restored on coinage at a ratio of 16 to 1 to gold in value, since that was the old standard before silver was devalued. He argued that the United States do so unilaterally as it had led in de-emphasizing silver as coinage. The effects would both be inflationary and still leave a stable precious bi-metal base under the American dollar.

Altgeld sold it to his party. It would be up to William Jennings Bryan to sell it to the nation.

Bryan had come to the convention an unknown Congressman from Nebraska. He was only 36 years old and probably had the cheapest hotel room of any delegate because he had less than $10 to pay for all his expenses.

The young Bryan was not the candidate favored by the Illinois governor, who so totally dominated the convention in other matters. Altgeld favored Richard Bland of Missouri and switched to Bryan only after he saw his candidate had no chance to win the nomination.

Bryan sparked the convention with the most famous speech ever given at a political convention.[6] It is remembered by the final line referring to those who would keep the country on the gold standard at all costs. He thundered, "You shall not crucify mankind upon a cross of gold."

For many who had been timid, his words made the monetary battle a righteous, if not a religious one.

His speech, however, contained several other points that reflected what was actually happening in the Democratic Party.

Bryan made a number of references to the East Coast and specifically to New York and Massachusetts, reminding them that others in the country "are equals before the law" with them and that the "merchant at the crossroads store is as much a businessman as the merchant of New York."

The rest of the nation, because it had Chicago and the strength of the Midwest, could stand up to the East. In one sense, Bryan was saying that New York was no longer as important as it had been economically and therefore it shouldn't be politically.

The fiery orator also talked of the shift in the party's allegiance primarily from the businessman to the worker. He argued that the term "businessman" would have to be redefined if it were to be part of the new political power base. The employee and the farmer would both have to be seen as businessmen.

Bryan raised the question:

> Upon which side shall the Democratic Party fight? Upon the side of the idle holders of capital, or upon the side of the struggling masses? That is the question that the party must answer first; and then it must be answered by each individual thereafter. The sympathies of the Democratic Party, as described by the platform, are on the side of the struggling masses, who have ever been the foundation of the Democratic party.7

It was radical talk for a presidential candidate in 1896.

William Jennings Bryan was defeated by William McKinley. The Republicans and the Cleveland Democrats were able to convince voters that possibly Bryan was a little too good of a talker, too much of an unknown. Some of their attacks on his depth and experience were well justified. Such did not detract from the credit that belongs to the man who formulated the silver issue and the Chicago Platform.

That platform also called for the government to promote the rights of workingmen, to restrain monopolies and to initiate an income tax.

The Republicans had very little trouble raising funds for the campaign, cashing in heavily both on many industrialists' opposition to such planks and on the business community's fear of Bryan and Altgeld.8

The Chicago Platform would again rise up as the "cause" in the 1900 convention and be a strong memory in 1904, but the country would have put much of its problem with deflation behind it by then and many of the Democrats' planks would become law in their own way. One of the reasons was that the Democrat's platform provisions were pushed even in city elections in the late 1890s. They were a creed which Altgeld was constantly evangelizing.9

The Populists, who had gotten a strong toehold with an independent Presidential candidate in 1892, endorsed Bryan in 1896, although they came up with their own vice-presidential candidate.

And, while Governor Altgeld did lead the Democratic Party to a position recognizing the needs and rights of the poor, which was more democratic, it would have many relapses. It would not be for another 36 years that the Democrats would rekindle a shadow of his spirit in the New Deal.

Altgeld, the democrat, died in 1902 and was buried along with Chicago's millionaires in Graceland Cemetery. He would die a publicly reviled man.

In Chicago there is a coterie of persons who still consider him the "Eagle Forgotten," the democrat who soared higher than any other.[10]

1. The Democratic Party of the nineteenth century was one which presented such presidential candidates as Stephen Douglas, George McClellan, Samuel Tilden and Grover Cleveland. Its theme was conservatism, first in the question of slavery and later; under Tilden and Cleveland, in financial and economic policies. This "conservatism" was tied into a laissez-faire policy toward large trusts and corporations, which in the pre-Sherman Anti-Trust days had become engulfing monopolies. For example, Cleveland's most famous use of the 1890 anti-trust legislation was against the American Railway Workers' Union in 1894.

2. Ray Ginger, "Altgeld's America" (Funk & Wagnalls, 1958) p.175. Other sources that support Ginger include: Allan Nevins in "Grover Cleveland: A Study in Courage" (1932) and Charles Warren in "The Manufacturer of History" (Stories From McClure's). Nevins says: "the silverites surged about the pale and taciturn Governor Altgeld, who might well have been nominated had not his foreign birth made him ineligible." Warren devotes 45 pages to a vivid description of Altgeld at work during the convention.

3. "The Chicago Platform of 1896" as it became known was not a liberal document by today's political standards. It was definitely conservative in comparison also to those of The National Party and the Populist Party in that same year (both also supported Bryan for president). For a contrast of them see "National Party Platforms: 1840 to 1960," compiled by Kirk Porter and Donald Johnson (1961). Altgeld's liberal views, on the other hand, were very deep and broad as illustrated by his governorship. With his espousing of the silver platform, he became principally a one-issue man and he made the Democratic Party that. It was the pivotal issue, one that those with wealth to protect could or would not espouse because it devalued their money. Instead of talking public health, schools, food programs, housing, etc., Altgeld's silver issue was a plan to put more money into the hands of the poor so they could buy the means to help meet these needs.

4. The telegrams, in edited form, were contained in a defense of his action that the then former President Grover Cleveland made at Princeton in 1904, "The Government in the Chicago Strike of 1894." Altgeld was dead at the time but Cleveland was anything but gracious in his comments.

5. Feelings at the convention were against not only Cleveland, but also New York and the East and were so strong as to be intemperate, according to Allan Nevins. "Animosity toward Eastern delegates," he stated, "was such that the slightest incident might have produced an explosion." On the other hand, Cleveland supporter Governor William E. Russell of Massachusetts went to Chicago with the avowed purpose of "saving the esprit de corps of the Eastern Democracy."

6. Bryan's speech is probably the most remembered purely political

speech in American annals. As such, it has been often memorized (without much comprehension) by student orators and studied by political scholars. The conclusions of the latter are that it was calculated, rehearsed endlessly, and honed so fine that it seemed both natural and effortless. History puts Bryan down as a three-time loser in his races for the presidency as well as an anachronism who sided against enlightenment and progress as Darrow's adversary in the Scopes Monkey trial in 1925. With that background, the speech is easily depreciated simply as an emotional crowd-pleaser. But, historically, it was far more. Combined with the situation at the convention that Altgeld had set up, it turned history in a different direction. Cleveland's biographer, Allan Nevins, wrote: "The gold men sat in sullen silence as pandemonium raged for thirty-five minutes after Bryan sat down. They sullenly answered to the roll-call as the platform was carried, 628 to 301, and the old Democratic Party, the party of Tilden and Cleveland, passed out of existence."

7. "Annals of America" Vol. 12, p.105.

8. *Harper's Weekly* magazine provided an example of the deeply angry and upset campaign that the Eastern and Republican forces waged against Bryan through Governor Altgeld. The magazine printed a cartoon near the end of the campaign that pictured Altgeld as resembling Charles Guiteau, who had in 1881 assassinated President Garfield. The caption read: "1881-1897: Guiteau was a Power in Washington for One Day. Shall Altgeld be a Power there for Four Years?" Harry Barnard in the "'Eagle Forgotten': The Life of John Peter Altgeld." (The Bobbs-Merrill Company, 1938) p.378 quotes from an editorial in *Harper's Weekly*:

> Gov. Altgeld...is the brain and inspiration of the movement for which Mr. Bryan stands...he preferred the impulsive, susceptible, imaginative, yielding Mr. Bryan...who would be as clay in the hands of the potter under the astute control of the ambitious and unscrupulous Illinois communist...To Gov. Altgeld the passage of a law establishing free coinage of silver would be but a step towards the general socialism which is the fundamental doctrine of his political belief...He seeks to overturn the old parties, the old traditions, and the essential policies which have controlled the government since its foundation.

9. The best blow-by-blow account of Altgeld's effort to keep the silver issue at the central point of American politics is contained in a rare booklet by W. F. Cooling, "The Chicago Democracy" (Platform Publishing Co., 1899).

10. The moving description of Altgeld as "The Eagle That Is Forgotten" comes from a poem honoring him that was written by Vachel Lindsay

"Collected Poems" (Macmillian, 1925) p.95. Some of the lines are particularly apt:

> They had snarled at you, barked at you, foamed
> at you, day after day.
> Now you were ended. They praised you,...and
> laid you away.

It ends:

> Sleep on, O brave-hearted, O wise man, that
> kindled the flame—
> To live in mankind is far more than to live
> in a name,
> To live in mankind, far, far more...than to live
> in a name.

The Black Power of Jack Johnson, Indignation Jones and Ida B. Wells

At the turn-of-the-century, 30,150 Chicagoans (1.9 percent of the city) were black, little different from the 1.1 percent figure in 1850. By 1910, the black population increased only to 2 percent or 44,103.

Still, from among that small minority, Chicago would glean some of its most dynamic, interesting and, in the long run, influential personages.

Unquestionably, the most famous of these was a man who opened a tavern on the South Side in 1911. He was Jack "Li'l Artha" Johnson, heavyweight boxing champion of the world from 1908 to 1915. Everything he represented was abhorrent to the "better" people and his activities were investigated by the Watch and Ward societies. He was, as a result, arrested in 1912 and charged with a violation of the Mann (white slavery) Act for bringing a woman across a state line for "immoral" purposes.

Viewed in the context of 1911 Chicago and America, Jack Johnson's life was the most explosive kind of protest. He had the opportunity to have all the things that were most forbidden him as a black man. He seized them with verve and gusto.

Johnson's nightclub was in the Levee or red light district of Chicago. The brothels, clubs and gambling houses there frequently employed black men as janitors, pianists, or night guards. Actually, their function was to serve often as the butt of jokes or simply to be patronized, a reminder to the insecure populace that there were members of a society "lower" and more desperate than they.

The heavyweight champion of the whole world, however, was "No. 1" in a sport that at the time was considered the most manly of all.[1] And he proved against one "great white hope" after another that he wasn't just a brute, but a clever man in the ring.

Furthermore, blacks could be tolerated when they were in church, but were to be totally condemned when they committed the sins which were considered the exclusive right of white men. Jack Johnson went out and "outsinned" them all.

The temptation is simply to brush off his life as superficial. It was, however, too deliberate and too stylized to be that easily ignored.

He once said,

> Friend...try anythin' once. Try it once and if you don't succeed, try something else. The fast life may be the short life, but it's the full life.[2]

After his first wife divorced him in 1910, he horrified the country more by publicly proclaiming his preference for white women. In Illinois, among other states, the legislature quickly tried to pass laws forbidding blacks to marry whites.

Jack Johnson salted his life with fast cars, women and gambling. Figures have been quoted of him spending $20,000 a week. Such "irresponsibility" came at a time when the most prominent black leader of the country, Booker T. Washington, was preaching extra measures of responsibility as the means for blacks to get into the American mainstream.

Johnson attempted to get free of the Mann Act indictment by marrying the principal witness against him, but it didn't help. He was sentenced to a year and a day in Leavenworth Prison. He jumped bond and fled to Paris. For two years he defended his title against European second-raters. Finally, on April 16, 1915, he lost his crown in a much-disputed fight with Jess Willard in Havana, Cuba. He later returned to the United States and served his prison sentence. He made several attempts at a comeback in the ring, including one at age 64. His full life was finally shortened by an accident in a car in which he was speeding. He was 68.

His life didn't win many civil rights battles, but it must have given no little satisfaction to a large number of blacks who were being stepped on by the righteous people. He became a symbol of pride to many in a impoverished black generation, just as Joe Louis would during the 1930s.[3]

A black contemporary of Jack Johnson's in Chicago, John G. Jones, was better known as "Indignation Jones." His was a far more deliberate effort to win civil rights battles. He, too, had no desire to follow Booker T. Washington's "self-help" strategy that seemed to accept the white's "separate but equal doctrine." The 1890s had been a very bad decade for blacks both in the South and the North, as they watched both laws and racial policies take away legal rights gained in the years following the Civil War. Few people were finding any means to fight the trend that was accentuated by the massive disenfranchisement of blacks and by a sharp increase in the number of lynchings.

The awesomeness of the task didn't stop Indignation Jones from trying. When there was a lynching, when there was a gross injustice, he called an "indignation meeting." A voice had to be heard. The city and the country's consciences had to be sensitized, even if they were not going to respond.

His protests were not merely against white racists, but also aimed at black leaders who he felt were not sensitive enough. He once brought together an indignation meeting against a coroner's jury which had handed down a verdict critical of integrated employment in a Chicago firm. Jones called for the jury to be tarred and feathered. He wasn't much easier on Booker T. Washington or even the prominent black Chicago physician, Dr. Daniel Williams.

Jones fought every form of segregation and was particularly active against a major effort made in 1903 to separate blacks and whites in Chicago schools. He subsequently was elected to and served in the state legislature.[4]

A man who attempted to have a foot both in Jack Johnson's and Indignation Jones' world was a black gambling house owner with the rather precious name of John V. "Mushmouth" Johnson. He ran some of the cheapest dives and had many of the most ruthless sluggers and "razor bucks" at his beck and call. He nevertheless contributed large sums to worthy causes, including churches. Because his money was so "tainted" he had to donate through others.[5]

Mushmouth Johnson's power, however, lay not in his toughs but in the money he accumulated. He once said, according to Gosnell: "While my family went in for religion and all that, I didn't exactly fancy so much book learning and went out to see where the money grew. Some of those who know me say I found it."[6]

Money for both Jack Johnson and Mushmouth Johnson was the great equalizer because it was what blacks, with few exceptions, so completely lacked. Mushmouth was not as free with his as Jack was, and the gambling house owner left over $200,000 to his sister at his death in 1907. His sister in turn married the wealthiest black businessman in Chicago, Jesse Binga. Their wealth was spent less on "worthy" causes, but it was used in 1908 to start the Binga Bank, an unheard of venture in black capitalism.

A black Chicagoan who was to become even wealthier and more influential nationally than Jesse Binga had started his business in 1905 on a capitalization of 25 cents. It was a newspaper he called the *Chicago Defender*. The man was Robert S. Abbott. The initial press run was 300 copies.

Other black newspapers existed in the city. The one with probably the most verve was the *Broad Ax*, edited by Julius F. Taylor. It was comparable to the *Chicago Times* in Storey's heyday as editor. It was economically radical, populist, a "preacher baiter" and referred to its enemies as "drunks, adulterers and thieves."

Taylor would have an impact, but the long term success story would be Abbott's. The difference to a large extent can be attributed to J. Hockley Smiley, who worked for the *Defender* from 1910 until his death in 1915. He had the marketing genius of an Aaron Montgomery Ward or a Richard Sears. He turned it into a newspaper to be reckoned with, creating both local and national editions. It became not only flamboyant, but also a clear voice of racial protest.

Like Deacon Bross of the *Chicago Tribune* and John Wright of the *Prairie Farmer* at the time of the Civil War, Abbott and the *Chicago Defender* "boomed" Chicago, encouraging large numbers of people to migrate to the city.

In the end, the *Defender*'s campaign would be very effective because Smiley's circulation system would reach into almost all of the black communities in the South and would talk of Chicago as the land of opportunity and of the high wages.

The *Chicago Defender* is well known for accelerating the migration of blacks from the South to the North and particularly to Chicago. That influx brought almost 50,000 blacks during World War I and then another 100,000 during the 1920s. The far greater cause of the migration, however, was the boll weevil, which almost completely destroyed the cotton crop of the South and drove southern blacks to actual starvation. It had started in Texas in 1892 and cut a swath across the South, ending in Georgia in 1915.

The *Defender* did far more than promote the move to Chicago.

According to Abbott's biographer, the paper reached a circulation during World War I of 283,000. To these subscribers and to its even larger number of additional readers, the paper expounded a philosophy. While not always militant or even consistent, it did promote racial pride, equality and rights. It favored protest, and that was radical for the southern black.[7]

The *Chicago Defender*, as with the other impetuses coming out of Chicago, was not a accident of fate. Smiley and Abbott had many Chicago prototypes in journalism, business and promotion to study to create their sensationally influential paper.

One of these from whom the *Defender* was able to learn was a black woman, a protester, and one-time journalist, Ida B. Wells. She married the city's foremost black attorney, Ferdinand L. Barnett. No one was tougher on Booker T. Washington and his accommodation theory than she was. She proclaimed that he was "largely responsible for the lynching in this country." She became the focus nationally of the anti-Booker T. Washington protest. The man she attempted to pull off his pedestal, however, was very firmly fastened to it. The Chicago group of protesters against him were not typical.[8] Others willingly took the self-dose of humiliating medicine he was inspiring blacks across the country to swallow.

Ida B. Wells was the only Chicago black among the original persons to call for the conference that led nationally to the founding of the NAACP. She stood alongside her good friend Jane Addams (who also had signed the "call" to organize it) in battling not only for racial equality, but also for suffrage and for help to meet the needs of the poor. Ironically, Chicago now has a large public housing project named "in her honor."

The *Defender* would present not nearly as sensitive a philosophy as did Ida B. Wells, but it did argue for dignity and against oppression. The bad words in the paper became "Jim Crow." It continued to harp against the separatis which Booker T. Washington was willing to accept.

Journalistically, according to Gosnell, the *Defender*'s model in many ways was the *Chicago Tribune*. Allan Spear in *Black Chicago*, however, claims it was William Randolph Hearst's *Chicago American*.

Both commentators were partly right. The *Defender*'s journalism imitated the *Tribune* and its sensationalism was acquired from the *American*. The *Defender* was proficient at both. Smiley was not above writing lurid and graphic lynch stories out of his head with datelines of little towns no one before or since ever heard of. On the other hand, just as the *Chicago Tribune* proclaimed itself the "World's Greatest Newspaper" and thus set a standard that made it look ridiculous if it did not live up to it, the *Chicago Defender* took as its motto, "The World's Greatest Weekly." As circulation grew and its purpose became clearer by the 1920s, it was able to build its own plant. No longer did it make up any of its news. And Robert Abbott found himself Chicago's first black millionaire.

The bitter and unfortunate experience of the black leaders of this era such as the Barnetts, Indignation Jones, Julius Taylor and Robert Abbott is that while they had the opportunity like Moses of leading people to the promised land, they had the additional experience of going into it and finding it wasn't flowing with milk and honey.

Still, they lived in a Chicago in which a large group of Chicagoans—black and white—experimented with the true ideas of a democracy. That was exciting and rewarding.

1. Johnson's autobiography, though stilted at times, gives us a lot more of the man than the play and movie of the late 1960s titled, "The Great White Hope." The play builds on the theme of bigotry against him, which he also discussed in his book. However, the theme of his autobiography (written in 1926), "Jack Johnson is Dandy" (Chelsea House Publishers, 1969) is more "try anything once." And Johnson did, from fighting anybody or anything (including a stint as a matador) to such stunts as trying to catch a greased razor-back pig or chasing a rabbit around a mile long course.

2. The quote is from Harry Sheer's column, "Voice of The Grand Stand." At the time (1946), it was appearing in the *Chicago Daily News.*

3. When Johnson did get out of prison, as he reports it, he was met by a crowd that included three bands.

4. "Indignation Jones" (John G. Jones) should not be confused with another famous black Chicago leader and politician John H. Jones, who in the late 1870s became the first Chicagoan of his race to hold county office (county commissioner). The life of "Indignation Jones" is synopsized in Allan Spear's "Black Chicago" (University of Chicago, 1967) p.62-3, while the story of John H. Jones can be found in "Negro Politicians: The Rise of Negro Politics in Chicago" by Harold F. Gosnell, (University of Chicago Press, 1935).

5. Mushmouth Johnson contributed anonymously to worthy causes through his mother, according to Gosnell. He also donated handsomely and equally to both parties, while encouraging blacks to register and vote. Interestingly enough, while Gosnell describes Johnson's career in detail and his various gambling activities, the book's index refers to him as "alleged gambling king."

6. *New York World* interview. July 25, 1907.

7. There are two good books on Abbott. One, "The Negro Press in the United States" by Frederick Detweiler (1922) quotes "one reputable Negro in Louisiana" as saying of the *Chicago Defender*, "My people grab it like a mule grabs a mouthful of fine fodder." The other is the biography of Abbott, "The Lonely Warrior: The Life and Times of Robert S. Abbott" (1955) by Roi Ottley.

8. Ida B. Wells, "Crusade for Justice" (University of Chicago, 1970) p.264. The black "leaders" or protesters in pre-World War I Chicago were closely related. Ida B. Wells was married to Ferdinand Barnett, who was the law partner of Indignation Jones. Their positions and determination were often little appreciated in their day. Ida B. Wells' autobiography, edited by her daughter, Alfreda Duster, speaks as much of protecting her flanks from petty criticism and put-downs by those around her as she does of the tough battles she fought against bigotry and lynchings.

Mail Order Democracy

Richard W. Sears and Aaron Montgomery Ward were two men who proved America wanted to buy Chicago.

The ads of these two men's mail order houses, and especially their catalogues, packaged the soul of Chicago and sent it through the mails and on the railroads reaching out like octopus arms from the city.

What was it they sold?

- The "good life" for pennies, and C.O.D.
- Steps on the ladder from drudgery to leisure, and consequently a culture that could have time to develop as a result of the sewing machines, cream separators, machinery, tool and household work-savers.
- A goal- or wish-oriented society in which people could dream of more freedom of choice in their lifestyles.
- More sensuality, a greater cultivation of tastes and a mass move away from a stimulus-deprived society represented by austerity, colorlessness and thrift.
- Cheap prices, quick delivery and a department store in your living room (or outhouse, as many kept their catalogues there).

Chicago became, as one *Tribune* reporter wrote, the "emporium" to the nation.1

On the other hand: A mail order house such as Sears, according to Jane Addams, was a "terrible place" to work. Unquestionably, assembly line working conditions in the mail order houses were, at times, brutal.

Retail merchants in small towns were so frustrated at the great swallowing up by the mushrooming Chicago mail order houses that they held catalogue burnings in public squares.

And, basically, the new "good life" was very materialistic.

Still, Richard Sears and Montgomery Ward were honorable men.[2] They were not monopolists of the public interests as were the robber barons of previous decades who had ruthlessly built trusts or cornered markets on the most basic of public needs such as gas, coal, oil, steel, transportation, sugar, power, grain, meat, and land. Sears and Ward set their prices in the marketplace, not by buying legislatures, city councils or cornering markets until they got the price they wanted.

The mail order houses sold directly to the people and used the Chicago style and resources to do it. These included: the city's railroads, immigrant labor, spirit and sensitivity to the "non-elite."

Motion picture studios today study the old mail order catalogues when they want to recreate that era on the screen. Several enterprises have reissued those "wish-books" just for the fascination value, as they so well recapture the period.

To appreciate more fully those catalogues, one has to read them sequentially and see the rapid change in goods from one to another, a revolution in products that they were helping to accelerate.[3]

A new, efficient, inexpensive cream separator, for example, was introduced into Sears Roebuck catalogue in 1905 for prices ranging from $31 to $39.[4] Competitors had been selling the same machine for $120 and most farmers could not afford one. They separated cream by hand or rushed milk to market every day without fail. Both were more time-consuming to the farmer than washing by scrub board was to the housewife. The result was that the farmers could feed the fresh skim milk to the stock and take the cream or butter to the creamery only two or three times a week.

And for the housewife, the two mail order giants provided a continuous parade of "new and improved" washing machines, stoves, sewing machines and similar work-saving devices. And they were being revolutionized. Both firms, incidentally, considered sewing machines their staple item. Sears had a whole separate catalogue of them and Ward saved the back page of his big book for sewing machine ads.

Ward's first catalogue appeared in 1872. Sears and Roebuck's came 20 years later, although Sears had started a mail order watch business in 1886. The biggest thrust for both occurred during the 1890s, especially between the Depression of 1893-96 and the one of 1907.

Company literature and histories of both firms make a strong point of how their founders "believed in the people, their customers."[5]

Prestigious businesses avoided the kind of customer that Sears and Wards catered to, the people who had little money and rarely a bank account. Large firms wanted purchasers when they could pay cash or establish solid credit. Otherwise, the companies wholesaled to small merchants, who could then worry about peoples' credit. The large department stores had been through enough Depressions to become very wary of credit purchases.

Sears showed a vigorous trust in people. He coined the selling phrase, "Send No Money." It appeared in all his ads, which showed up in every local, small newspaper and magazine in the country. They told people to order what they wanted, to look it over and, if not satisfied, to send it back at no cost.

The farmers and the poor of the country had just been through a Depression (1893-96) in which even many of their best friends and relatives had not trusted them in financial transactions. Suddenly, they were being told by a large company, "You don't have to trust us because we trust you." Sears also often threw in three-week trial periods.

And the companies introduced guarantees. One writer described Richard Sears penchant for guarantees:

> While Richard Sears did not invent the idea of a guarantee, he blew it up to fantastic proportions. He guaranteed not only that the sewing machine would sew and sew satisfactorily, but that it would sew better than any other sewing machine in the world. He guaranteed the bobbin, the shuttle, the treadle, the leather belt for the treadle. He guaranteed the solid oak cabinet, the varnish and linseed oil, used to bring out the grain. He guaranteed the machine would arrive safely and that the neighbors would admire it once they were permitted to inspect it.
>
> He guaranteed the man's suit at $4.50 to be heavyweight, strictly all wool. He guaranteed its lining, trimmings, buttons and buttonholes.[6]

Sears got returns and complaints. At one time, for example, his firm was selling 10,000 women's hats a week and getting back 1,500.

Complaints and correspondence sometimes bogged down the staff but the firm established its reputation on keeping such pledges. Annually, the returns, over all, averaged less than 4 percent.

Aaron Montgomery Ward had also built his firm upon recognition and respect for customers who were not rich and affluent. Ward had been in the mail order business two decades before Sears and Alva C. Roebuck became partners. He had also stressed the guarantee on his products, but even more important in the 1870s and 1880s had made use of the farmers' very strong national union of the late 1880s, the Grange. Members of it received special attention and orders sent via a Grange official or countersigned with the Grange seal did not have to be paid for upon receipt but had a ten day grace period. Ward's catalogues carried on the covers, "The Original Grange Supply House."

Montgomery Ward & Co. is acknowledged to be the world's first mail order supply house.[7] Its founder had been a clerk in the Field and Leiter store in Chicago and a salesman in small towns. When he started his "buy in large quantities and sell directly through the mail at low prices" company, he hit upon the ingredients the poorer classes were most eager to pay for: trust, faith and above all respect. A. Montgomery Ward sold them first his slogans, "Your money back if not satisfied" and "You can't go wrong if you deal with Montgomery Ward" and only then, his merchandise.

Other giant Chicago mail order firms followed his patterns, developing thicker catalogues each year just as Ward did. Spiegel and May Stern Co. was begun in Chicago in 1882 and the Cloak and Suit Co. (later National Bellas Hess), in 1888.

Richard Sears had started a mail order watch company in 1886 on a shoestring and sold his firm three years later for $72,000. Alva C. Roebuck, a watchmaker, became first Sears' employee in the R.W. Sears Watch Co. and later his partner in founding the A.C. Roebuck Co. It issued its first catalogue in 1891. In 1893, the name was changed to Sears, Roebuck and Company and the base of its operation shifted from Minneapolis to its new offices in Chicago. In that same year, it came out with a 332-page catalogue.

By Richard Sears' death in 1908, the firm was able to claim sales larger than the next five largest mail order houses combined, including Wards.

Sears was the driving force of the new company, although he also took in such men as Julius Rosenwald and Max Adler, who more than competently carried on the firm after his drive and push wilted in the 1907 Depression. Roebuck sold his minor interest in the growing firm.[8]

No one, however, was able to duplicate Sears' feats in propelling the firm from $137,000 in sales in 1891 to $50,000,000 in 1907.

His promotional gimmicks, advertising techniques, methods of distribution, guarantees, slogans and business acumen were all factors, but to put the emphasis on them is to take the credit away from the people who found his firm a good place to get quality merchandise much cheaper than anywhere else. He understood the small town and rural American, but they also understood him. They liked someone who talked their simple language (immigrants found instructions in their languages also). They liked someone who advertised in their magazines and local newspapers as Sears did. But, most of all, they chose the firm which let them see the product first and stuck to its guarantees.

Sears occasionally betrayed the trust the people put in him. His line of patent medicines was the worst example. His catalogues often led off with ads for such "cures" as "Dr. Echol's Cure for Heart Trouble," "Dr. Wilden's Quick Cure for Indigestion and Dyspepsia" and "Brown's Vegetable Cure for Female Weakness." Ward, on the other hand, was tamer in his claims and spoke of "remedies" rather than "cures." The Pure Food and Drug Act of 1906 and muckrakers of the day helped trim the claims of both firms. Between 1896 and 1905, Sears also sold over $400,000 worth of "electric belts," according to Boris Emmet and John E. Jeuck in their book, "Catalogues and Counters." The belts were meant to achieve many of the same purposes as the cure-all patent medicines. While Sears, Roebuck and Company was getting an average of 8 to 10 percent profits on its sales, it was annually collecting 45 to 68 percent gross and 28 to 31 percent net profits on electric belt sales.

Richard Sears' successor, Julius Rosenwald, is well acknowledged for his philanthropy especially among blacks and in the Jewish community. Neither he nor Sears, however, showed the consideration for employees that their customers generally received in those early days. An early general manager of the firm, prodded by an encounter with Jane Addams, made some inroads in company policy toward its workers, but the mail order warehouses remained just slightly above sweatshops in working conditions.[9] These have been poignantly described in Halper's 1930s novel, "The Chute."

Nonetheless, Aaron Montgomery Ward,[10] Richard Sears and the other Chicago mail order giants rode a vast strong wave that flooded out from Chicago and across America. The goods, products and luxuries that composed that wave had never before been considered to be the "just deserts" of the small farmer, factory worker and small tradesman. As a result, Chicago—through its giant mail order houses—helped partially to democratize the material aspects of the new American culture.

1. The *Chicago Tribune* was an early vehement critic of mail order houses, according to Boris Emmet and John Jeuck in their monumental history of Sears, Roebuck and Company, "Catalogues and Counters" (University of Chicago, 1950) p.151-2.

2. In November, 1873, the *Tribune* warned, "Grangers Beware: Don't Patronize Montgomery Ward & Co.—they are Dead-Beats." The paper, whose revenues came from local merchants, argued that patrons of the company are "gulls," "credulous fools," and "dupes." The *Tribune* completely retracted a month later, but the authors claim it had set "the tone for many subsequent attacks on mail order." Emmet and Jeuck point out that many newspapers, for decades, remained highly critical of the large mail order houses and helped promote "Home-Trade Clubs" to encourage people to buy from local merchants.

3. By way of contrast, there was William Vanderbilt's "The public be damned" or George Pullman's edict to his workers "nothing to arbitrate." Richard Sears was as outgoing as the most facile of traveling salesmen and Montgomery Ward built his firm on the gregariousness of the Granger movement.

4. Various old catalogues in the 1970s were republished by the Gun Digest Publishing Company. Among them are: the 1908 Sears, Roebuck & Co., the 1894-95 Montgomery Ward & Co. and the 1896 Marshall Field & Co. Jewelry and Fashions catalogues.

5. According to Louis Asher in his early history of Sears, Roebuck & Co., "Send No Money" (Argus, 1942), a cream separator had been listed in an early (probably 1903) catalogue, but there had not been one single order for it. A modicum of success followed one subsequently listed for $62.50. Sears himself, visiting a farm in North Dakota, saw the importance to the farmer of a cream separator and bought half-interest in a factory in order to sell them inexpensively. The machine's sales became not only a bulwark in the company's stability, but also the key to Sears' highly successful "Iowaizing" scheme. In it, farmers sent in names of farmers who might need cream separators. If they bought them, the person who submitted the names earned premiums. In the first half of 1908, according to Emmet and Jeuck, "roughly $1,000,000 worth of cream separators were sold, returning a net profit of $300,000—about one-quarter of the entire profits of Sears, Roebuck and Co. in that period."

6. The language of the mail order houses was crucial. Richard Sears wrote all his own advertising copy at the onset, according to Louis Asher (who was Sears' "man Friday" at the time). As the company expanded and he occasionally couldn't write a piece, Sears would edit the ad heavily to make it "homespun and forthright." Asher states that Sears won his customers "by speaking their language, a common language of practical understanding and

plain talk." While others—especially educators—were depreciating the Midwest's vernacular, Sears was creating rapport and trust simply by using it in communications with his potential buyers.

7. This quote is also from Louis Asher's well-done book (much of the writing is attributable to co-author, Edith Heal), p. 55. Unfortunately, the book is not indexed.

8. The idea of the guarantee in the development of both Wards and Sears is stressed in all the historical material about the firms.

9. "Catalogues and Counters," while subtitled "A History of Sears, Roebuck and Co." is a thorough 778-page piece of scholarship that is probably also the most objective history of Sears biggest competitor, Montgomery Ward's. The authors constantly compare the two firms, both in growth and policies. Montgomery Ward & Co. issued its own history, "1872-1972: A Century of Serving Consumers" by Frank B. Latham, available from the firm's public relations office.

10. Alva Roebuck in later years argued that he—as a deeply religious man—separated from Sears because of a difference in ethics. Emmet and Jeuck, however, say that Roebuck's health and his fear of the company's liability caused him to sell out in 1895. (P.47) He was hired by the firm in the 1930s for promotional and public relations reasons. One of these was that since the 1890s, a rumor had been spread in the South that Alva Roebuck was black. He was sent there to make personal appearances, a fellow employee from the 1930s told this author. The rumor is still occasionally heard.

11. Chicago has yet to see a more generous philanthropist than Julius Rosenwald. His memorials include the Museum of Science and Industry in Chicago and fantastically large donations to black education in the South and to worthy charities, especially Jewish ones in Chicago. Nevertheless, his pay scales for employees, particularly in the early days of the firm, were far from generous. The Illinois Vice Commission in 1916 summoned him to testify on the wages paid young women in his employ. Wages for girls at the time were as low as $5 a week and 1,465 women employees at Sears were earning less than $8 a week. Chicago historian Finis Farr in "Chicago: A Personal History of America's Most American City" (Arlington House, 1973) p.299, commented: "Julius Rosenwald had offered no competition to the vice lords for services of women and girls." See also the "Report of the Senate Vice Committee: State of Illinois" (1916) . M.R. Werner in his 1939 biography "Julius Rosenwald" (Harper & Brothers, 1939) treats his subject with praise, honor and respect.

12. If Rosenwald's memorial is the Museum of Science and Industry, Ward's is Chicago's unobstructed lakefront in Grant Park. Ward fought legal battles as far as the State Supreme Court to keep the land, as in its deed, "forever open, clear, and free." One of his opponents was the board of directors of the Field Museum, who threatened not to build unless the structure could be put

up in Grant Park. It subsequently was erected just south of the park. Another opponent was the Burnham Plan, the 1909 comprehensive plan for Chicago, which time has been carelessly immortalized. It called for buildings in Grant Park, specifically museums. Ward fought heavy criticism to achieve what is recognized as a simple, beautiful quality of the city today. Lois Wille tells his story in "Forever Open, Clear and Free" (Henry Regnery Company, 1972).

Saloon versus Salon Politics

Unquestionably, Chicago's most notorious "product" ever was the gangsterism of the 1920s. Several generations later, a native Chicagoan can go few places in the world without hearing a voice uttering the rat-a-tat of a machine gun or the name Al Capone in response to the name of Chicago.

Historians and social analysts will long argue the various reasons that bootlegging and gangs were so prominent in Chicago during the twenties.

An obvious part of the answer is the publicity Al Capone and other mobsters have received. "The Guinness Book of World Records", for example, claims he earned more than $100 million a year, a figure way out of proportion with the court records used to prosecute him for income tax evasion. Trial records indicate that, more likely, Capone made about $8 to $10 million in 1927. Guinness gives no source to establish what the government couldn't.

Another very important reason for Capone's rise goes back to the turn-of-the-century and the unique success in Chicago of "municipal reform."

The link between the two was a man who served as a "municipal reformer" alderman in the early 1900s and then in the 1920s as the mayor whom Al Capone owned. He was Big Bill Thompson. There were other connections.

The transition from the reform movement in Chicago to the even more successful alliance between crime and politics in the 1920s represents a sorry but understandable era in Chicago history.[1]

Certainly, one of the least known facts of the city's history is that it once received national attention as the town that had rooted out corruption. Chicago alone achieved one of the most written about American goals at the turn-of-the-century, "municipal reform."

In the early 1900s, Lincoln Steffens—the most famous of all the "muckraker" journalists—visited Chicago. His purpose was to expose political corruption in the city as he had so successfully done in Philadelphia and New York. The *McClure's Magazine* series eventually was published as his famous book, "The Shame of the Cities."[2]

Chicago startled Steffens. He wrote of it in his autobiography:

> My mental diagram of "the" American city fitted Chicago, but it was out of joint. The machine didn't work; the bosses were in trouble.
>
> Who was the boss of Chicago? Nobody, they said. Who owned the mayor? Nobody. Who controlled the city council? The Voters League, a reform organization!
>
> From a journalistic point of view, the exhibition of Chicago as something for other cities to imitate was a sensation; it was more astonishing "news" than the graft article which I had meant to write could possibly have been. Here was the way to do it and other cities did follow Chicago's lead. That is to say, they set up Municipal Voters Leagues, and sure enough, some of them got results; not good government, not normal representative government, but—a temporary betterment.[3]

Steffens explains that this reform in Chicago didn't end crime in the streets, commenting that "The New York Tenderloin was a model of order and virtue compared with the badly regulated, police-paid criminal lawlessness of the Chicago Loop." It did help defeat Charles T. Yerkes. The latter was trying to bribe his way to a perpetual stranglehold on the city's streetcar lines. What it was most successful doing was replacing "conscientious" businessmen for aldermen willing to take "boodle" (graft).

In the years after his visit to Chicago, Steffens came to realize that the revolution in the city's power structure was perhaps more of a warning than it was a model for future municipal reform.[4]

The form of government he actually witnessed in Chicago was, in his words, an "aristocratic democracy." Steffens described its basic purpose: "It was just what big business said it wanted, a government that understands and is just to business."[5] Ultimately, this very narrow base upon which the "reform" was built was the reason it failed.

This was the same reason that in the midst of the "reform" the city's social conscience, Jane Addams, was turned off to it. Why Clarence Darrow literally laughed Steffens out of his office as "the man who believes in honesty." And why former Governor John Peter Altgeld, when he attempted to to run for mayor of Chicago on a platform of social reform, was defeated partially by "municipal reform."

The reformers came to believe that "honesty" was enough, that they didn't need representative government or a social conscience. They simply didn't understand. They didn't have room for democracy the way Louis Sullivan, Francis Parker, John Peter Altgeld, Eugene Debs, Jane Addams or the other Chicago who believed did.

The man who started their reform, however, was a believer in democracy, at least to a greater extent than those who followed him. He was William T. Stead, who gave a series of lectures on Chicago at the Central Music Hall in 1894, prior to publishing them in his book "If Christ Came to Chicago." His belief was that conditions could be changed in the city. He spoke graphically of the need to feed the hungry and pointed out that the corrupt politicians were giving out food in their saloons. He talked of sheltering the homeless and reported a police force on the take was housing the homeless in precinct stations overnight.[6]

His exposé in 1894 of how "boodling" was handled in the city council stands as a classic piece of political reporting that has probably been unmatched in Chicago since. In the long run, it was the only part of his challenge that the business community would take to heart. He wrote:

> It is necessary, if you wish to get anything through the council, to "square" the alderman. The "squaring" is done discreetly and with due regard to the fundamental principle which sums up the whole law of the boodler, namely: thou shalt not be found out. If it is a small thing, such as an ordinance sanctioning a projection over the street, it is not necessary to square more than one alderman. This can be done directly or through an intermediary. In all cases, however, the alderman must be "seen." Remittances through the

post are discouraged; bank checks are at a discount; the transaction takes place in the presence of no third party, but face to face. If it is a very small matter a trifle will suffice, for your alderman is not above small pickings by the way. It is very different matter, however, when the question is one involving a railway franchise or a new gas ordinance. Then much more elaborate machinery is employed. The council is sometimes divided and redivided into various rings. In the present council one alderman who usually can be found in the neighborhood of Powers & O'Brien's saloon, can control forty others. The head of the big ring is the boss. There is also a smaller ring which, as the larger, has its own chief.

When a franchise is applied for, or in other words something is proposed to be stolen from the city, it is necessary to ascertain on what terms the alderman will consent to hand the stolen goods out of the windows of the City Hall. For carrying on such negotiations, the first desideratum is a safe man, one who can be depended upon not to take more than a certain proportion of the swag. This gentleman is usually outside the council, but he commands the confidence of both parties to the transaction.

He is the go-between, and all transactions are conducted by him by word of mouth. He seeks the head of the ring to ascertain whether the boys are hungry and with how little they can be induced to stand "pat." Into the conferences between the go-between and the boys the world is not admitted. The secrets of a papal conclave are not more sacredly preserved than the details of the conferences between the chiefs of the corrupt ring in the City Hall and the corporations who are in for the deal. As both parties mean business they arrive at an understanding, and the money, whether it be $500, $750, $1,000 or $1,500, is agreed upon. An ordinance, usually drawn up by the corporations which proposes the steal, is entrusted to one of the gang, who introduces it with such garnishings as he deems desirable. If the franchise is not very objectionable on the face of it, it usually goes through. Alderman are bound to oblige each other and as the city property has been chucked away every month without any protest, it is quite possible for the ordinance to pass without serious debate. If, on the other hand, there are any of the aldermen who have been left out in the cold in the promised distribution of the boodle, there may be a debate with heated discussion. Sometimes, of course, this opposition may be perfectly genuine and due to the natural indignation of honest men against a barefaced swindle. But even when this is the case, the opposition is generally aided by one or more of the boodling alderman who oppose the ordinance with a view of putting up their price.

This maneuver is very familiar in the City Council. It is discounted by the manager of the ring, who knows the price of his boys as well as the farmer knows the price of his hogs.

The precise number of boodlers in the City Council is a question upon which there is often much discussion. A lawyer of a railway corporation, speaking on the subject the other day, said, "There are sixty-eight aldermen in the city council and sixty-six of them can be bought. This I know because I have bought them myself." This was probably a little exaggerated bluff on his part. No other authorities put the percentage of non-boodling aldermen so low as this, I have gone through the list of the aldermen repeatedly, with leading citizens, both inside the council and outside, journalists, ministers and men of business. The highest estimate of non-boodlers that I have heard was eighteen out of sixty-eight. Between the minimum of two and the maximum of eighteen it will probable not err on the side of charity if we admit that there are ten aldermen on the Council who have not sold their votes or received any corrupt consideration for voting away the patrimony of the people.[7]

Stead's account was the classic story of big city corruption. It was being repeated around the country, especially in New York's Tammany Hall politics.

The British journalist investigated deeply enough, however, to see that the most needy of the city often got immediate rewards through their aldermen and precinct captains in such a system. It could be meted out in patronage jobs, a few dollars at election time, free lunches in saloons, a fix in court, help in becoming citizens, a pass on a building code violation and assistance in getting city services. What to the businessman seemed an "efficient" municipal government could ignore all these needs for poorer citizens. And the reform government of Chicago, that Steffens witnessed and praised, did ignore problems. In that vacuum of not meeting the little needs, Chicago would elect Big Bill Thompson mayor in 1915 and then reelect him again in 1919 and 1927. He would restore machine politics to Chicago for generations.

The original plan for reform in Chicago called for the type of democratic representation that could avoid some of the problems. The Civic Federation, conceived in the 1880s by the socially aware First National Bank President Lyman Gage, became a reality as a result of Stead's Central Music Hall speeches. It was a very broad organization with the following departments: philanthropic, industrial, educational, moral and political. Committee members included such famous wealthy Chicagoans as Marshall Field, Cyrus McCormick, Jr. and Harlow Higinbotham as well as social crusaders Jane Addams, Graham Taylor (of Chicago Commons) and Albion W. Small, social thinker from the newly founded University of Chicago.

The Civic Federation in 1894 and 1895 began to carry out Stead's dream. It organized relief-work among the hungry, cleaned up the city's streets (raising private funds to help), fought grafting garbage contractors, led an ax and crow-bar assault on gambling and got its feet wet in politics.[8]

The Civic Federation was acutely aware of the boodling city council. Initial efforts to defeat the more corrupt alderman brought only two or three victories. Conferences were held in 1895 of 200 prominent business leaders from the Civic Federation, City Club and other organizations to come up with a plan to defeat the boodlers and replace them with conscientious "taxpayers." Various plans were argued, including the formation of a third party, new state legislation and more study.

The group wanted action. The 1896 aldermanic elections would be ripe. Charles T. Yerkes must be defeated along with his effort to bribe the council into extending his control of the city streets by getting more and longer term franchises for streetcar lines. He had already collared the Loop with the ghastly "L" structure.

A small committee was selected and they in turn chose a man to fight the battle. He was George Cole, variously described as a "bulldog" and a "buzz saw" of a man. The organization which the committee created to support him was named the Municipal Voters League. It was born Feb. 12, 1896.

George Cole was a small stationery store owner who considered himself a "second-class businessman." He was tenacious and at his best in a scrap. He had to contend with a libel suit and threats on his family, but he won unbelievable victories.

Cole could not be bought, pushed or pressured, even though a number of the founding members of the group eventually tried to do so. His organization set out to expose the boodlers, naming names and writing up long lists of suspicious or obviously bought votes. On the other hand, this new crusade made it fashionable for wealthy businessmen to run for aldermen. Bertha Palmer even offered up her son, Honore, for aldermanic office, holding precinct worker teas in her North Lake Shore Drive castle.[9] Joan Miller's study of the candidates who were eventually supported by the Municipal Voters League described them as "more Republicans than Democrats, more Protestants than Catholics, more wealthy and middle class than working class candidates."

Statistics are a little deceptive when one attempts to distinguish the kinds of professions. The League, for example, supported 26 candidates who were businessmen and opposed in various elections 29 businessmen. Of the latter, however, 12 were saloon owners. The educational background is indicative of the distinctions the organization matter of factly made:[10]

	League-supported men	League-opposed men
College or further	33	8
Business school	3	3
Trade school	1	1
High school	4	6
Common school	9	19
Unknown	0	13

The 1896 battle results were phenomenal. Cole claimed the election of 27 good aldermen out of 36 (only half of the council had been up for election). He felt he could count on 6 of the left-over aldermen. It seemed enough to sustain a veto against Yerkes' paid-for legislation to extend his franchises. The final confrontation would come later and would require even the votes of First Ward Aldermen Hinky Dink Kenna and Bathhouse John Coughlin, both of whom otherwise were the classic enemies of the League.

The story is told of an earlier encounter between Cole and Coughlin, the red-light district alderman. Coughlin stormed into the League's office to protest a copy of his background and record that had been distributed to show his nefarious deeds. It was not right, he said. Cole offered to change any inaccuracy and subsequently did. Coughlin's sole objection, it turned out, was that the record stated he was born in Waukegan whereas he had first seen the light in Chicago, a fact of which he was particularly proud.11

Many reform aldermen never stood for reelection. A few others got "grafted" over to the other side. Still the boodlers were so cut off from revenue for a while that they were compared to "gray wolves" hungrily looking in from the outside. The name stuck.

Others succeeded George Cole and the Municipal Voters League remained a strong, active power block in the city until the early 1920s. Its techniques included publicly shaming the gray wolves to the point where their families would urge them to quit. It also used compromise, back room meetings and trade-offs

Writing in 1902, Jane Addams excoriated this limited concept of politics by the reformers:

> The well-to-do men of the community think of politics as something off by itself...As a result of this detachment, "reform movements" started by businessmen and the better element are almost wholly occupied in the correction of political machinery and with a concern for the better method of administration, rather than with the ultimate purpose of securing the welfare of the people. They fix their attention so exclusively on methods that they fail to consider the aims of city government.12

Commenting on ward bosses from out of her experience, she said,

> They are corrupt and often do their work badly; but they at least avoid the mistake of a certain type of businessmen who are frightened by democracy and have lost faith in the people.[13]

During the late 1890s there was a candidate for office in Chicago who represented the form of democracy in which Jane Addams believed. He was the former governor of Illinois, John Peter Altgeld. He ran for mayor in 1898 against Carter Harrison II, who had gained considerable strength among voters. Harrison made inroads among the reformers because of his veto of the Yerkes bill. Harrison, Altgeld said, claimed to be a Democrat, a member of the party whose presidential candidate, Bryan, was crying that the poor were being "crucified upon a cross of gold." Yet the incumbent mayor had openly sold Chicago city bonds as gold bonds, thus angering those who felt the gold standard helped the wealthy and hurt the poor.

Altgeld, although physically sick, pushed his frustrating election campaign effort because he wanted to promote the democratic issues he deeply believed in.[14] He suffered the bitter enmity of the business community, being considered an anarchist by both it and the press because he had pardoned the remaining men convicted in the Haymarket trial. He lost the election, getting more than 40,000 votes, even though it was said that there was not in the pockets "of all the Altgeld committee the price of one square meal."

Unfortunately, too many extraneous factors had been involved in Altgeld's campaign for it to have succeeded to the degree that the Municipal Voters League oligarchy did.

When Big Bill Thompson first ran for mayor in 1915, by contrast, the reformers were not strongly against him. He was one of the rich young men who had been persuaded to run for alderman. He was president of the Chicago Yacht Club and had been captain of the Chicago Athletic Club football team. They commented, "The worst that can be said of him is that he isn't very smart."[15]

Within two years much worse things were being said. The strongest was that he had systematically subverted and sabotaged the Chicago school system by appointing incompetents to the Board of Education and then had cut down on the number of board members to avoid pressure to add qualified board members.

Thompson was reelected twice as mayor of Chicago. The second time (1927) happened despite tremendous scandals and a fairly open allegiance with the gangsters, Capone in particular. The reformers were completely bewildered by how he accomplished it. The answer, however, was fairly simply. He was elected by the little people (in terms of money, education and power) whose interests and felt needs had been neglected by the reformers. This particularly included the long-snubbed black community.

As a result, Thompson got to be mayor of Chicago for a total of 12 years and was able to stuff his desk drawers and other out-of-the-way places with $2,103,024 by the time he died in 1944.[16] Most of it was in gold certificates.

1. This chapter is also meant to give a background view of the subsequent control of "machine" politics in Chicago and Cook County. The Democratic organization dominated the city's politics in the person of Mike McDonald for 20 years after The Chicago Fire (1871). His political demise in the mid-1890s helped create the vacuum that "reform" partially filled. Alderman Paddy Bauler's famous 1940s quote "Chicago ain't ready for reform" could, with a little historical perspective, be rephrased, "Chicago tried reform harder than anybody else and it failed." The Republicans and the independents 100 years later merely seem to be trying to repeat the mistakes the "reformers" made in the 1890s, forgetting that the interests of more people seem to be vested in the neighborhood saloon than in the high-rise coffee party. The best study in the matter is Harold F. Gosnell's "Machine Politics: Chicago Model" (University of Chicago, 1937).

2. The thesis for this chapter basically rests on a triangulation of three sources: One is an unpublished thesis at Roosevelt University by Joan Miller "The Politics of Municipal Reform in Chicago During The Progressive Era: The Municipal Voters League As a Test Case" (1966) that statistically and brilliantly analyzed Chicago's turn-of-the-century reform movement. (A copy is available at the Newberry Library). The Second is the Chapter in Lincoln Steffens' autobiography (Harcourt, Brace & Co., 1931) about his visit to the "reformed" Chicago and the third is "If Christ Came to Chicago," a book we quote extensively throughout this and other chapters. Also helpful was George Cole's biography, "Citizen Cole" by Hoyt King (self-published, 1931), "Lords of the Levee," "Big Bill of Chicago" and "Come Into My Parlor," all cited earlier.

3. Steffens, op. cit. p.423.

4. The positive to negative view of Chicago in Steffens' autobiography comes from the fact that he first talks of his immediate impressions of the city when he visited in the early 1900s and which he wrote up in *McClure's* magazine. His autobiography was written in 1931, by which time he had a chance to see the direction the reformers had, by then, moved in. Disillusion clearly had set in for Steffens.

5. Steffens, p.429.

6. The newspapers, which Stead had set on the seat of their pants by his thorough reporting work in Chicago, tried to brush off his book. The *Chicago Herald* said "This book contains nothing that is novel." The *Chicago Tribune* called it "obscene" and said it "ought to be suppressed." The *Chicago Dispatch* said it was "flat," "stale," "libelous" and "scurrilous." The *Inter-Ocean* stated that "it is certain to give the enemies of Chicago occasion to blaspheme." These quotes appear at the end of the British edition.

7. Stead, op. cit. p.177.

8. The distinction between what Stead and Gage conceived to be the political reform movement with a broad base and the limited one that was

achieved is important. See Lloyd Lewis and Henry Justin Smith, "Chicago, the History of Its Reputation" (Harcourt, Brace & Co., 1929) p.243 ff.

9. Bertha Honore Palmer also served as vice-president of the Civic Federation. It was in a day, of course, when women couldn't even vote in Illinois.

10. These statistics are from Joan Miller's thesis, cited at the beginning of the chapter. She did the research.

11. The story is told in Hoyt King's "Citizen Cole" p.47. The author of the biography worked with Cole in the Civic Federation.

12. "Democracy and Social Ethics" (Macmillan, 1907) p.222. Jane Addams later in the book spoke much more highly of the precinct captains whom she often had to fight than of the philanthropists, who gave considerable financial backing to Hull House.

13. "Democracy and Social Ethics" p.222.

14. There was an excellent statement of Altgeld's political beliefs about municipal democracy distributed at the time of the election, W. F. Cooling's "The Chicago Democracy." Altgeld believed that democracy was THE issue both for the national party and for municipal elections. He believed it so strongly that any compromisers (such as Carter Harrison II) and other city politicians in a number of other cities became the enemy even though they were fellow Democrats.

15. One of the most lively books ever written about Chicago is "Big Bill of Chicago" (Bobbs-Merrill Company, 1953) by Lloyd Wendt and Herman Kogan. The following quote by the two authors helps show why: "'Bill Thompson's the man for me!' sang some, and others answered, "He has the carcass of a rhinoceros and the brain of a baboon!' Some cried, 'Big Bill's heart is as big as all outdoors!' and others replied, 'The people have grown tired of this blubbering jungle hippopotamus!'" p.12.

16. "Big Bill of Chicago," p.358.

Chicago Molds a Man, Clarence Darrow

Before Clarence Darrow, the nation's legal system in the immigrant-packed cities tended to be a bully used to whip into line the poor, working people, protesters and foreign-speaking. Courts run by the likes of Judge (later Governor) John Peter Altgeld were extremely rare. Afterwards, it would not always work that way quite as easily. Darrow had spit in the bully's eye and had repeatedly come away the winner from the ensuing scrap. He had set the important American legal precedent that the little guy didn't always have to lose.

The "little guy" in many cases won only because the system allowed for the "fix." Politicians such as Aldermen Bathhouse John Coughlin and Hinky Dink Kenna derived not a little of their power because they could provide bail bond, counsel and often favorable judicial rulings for their constituents. An irate description of the two aldermen at work in court is given in "Chicago and Its Cess-Pools of Infamy" by Samuel Paynter Wilson (1909). Speaking of them, Wilson wrote:

> These two men (and I do not single them out by any personal ill-feeling, but merely because they represent a type of politician prevalent in the great cities where vice and poverty exist) are known to a certain portion of the citizens of that ward as "good fellows."

The ultimate abuse of the courts, however, had been the Haymarket trial in Chicago on June 21, 1886. A person unknown (probably Rudolph Schnaubelt, never brought to trial) threw a bomb at a group of police attempting to break up an anarchist rally in Haymarket Square. Four peaceful men were hanged for "aiding, abetting, advising and encouraging" Schnaubelt through a "conspiracy." It was never established that he threw the bomb or why the person (whoever tossed it) did so. How, therefore, it could be established they had "aided, abetted, advised or encouraged" such a person was a question left unanswered in the wake of a rush to use the courts to end the "anarchist menace" to the establishment. More complex treatment of the question can be found in a compilation of original source material: "The Chicago Haymarket Riot: Anarchy on Trial" (D. C. Heath and Company, 1959) by Bernard Kogan, or in "The History of the Haymarket Affair" (Farrar & Rinehart, 1936) by Henry David.

By nature, Clarence Darrow was not the man for the job. He was possibly the greatest cynic since Voltaire, saying of the world, "It's all a big bughouse. I'll be glad to leave it."[1]

By heritage, however, he had little choice. The human who was like his father was John Peter Altgeld; the loving person to whom he was a bonded brother was Eugene Debs and his actual legal partner was Edgar Lee Masters. And you would have to name as mother to this man, Chicago.

Darrow was already a lawyer and past 30 when he arrived in Chicago in 1888 from Ashtabula, Ohio. He had not proved himself in any way a spectacular lawyer. He had an interest in, but not a burning zest for, the issues of justice and democracy. Even his desire for reading and knowledge lay dormant.

Still, it was a book that Darrow had read in Ashtabula that inevitably changed his life. That volume was "Our Penal Machinery and Its Victims" by John Peter Altgeld, then a Chicago judge. The writings were revolutionary to the practising attorney. Altgeld, who had made some money in Chicago real estate, had paid for the first printing of 10,000 copies and had sent them out to every judge, magistrate, warden, educator, lecturer and social service he could find on any mailing list.

The two men met in Chicago in 1889 and, of that relationship, Irving Stone has written:

> The 40-year-old Altgeld was the profoundest influence in Darrow's life. He helped educate the younger man, buttressed in him his love of study, of acquiring all the facts no matter how distasteful they might appear, of clinging steadfastly to the truth even in the face of such devastating tempests as were nearly to destroy both men before their lives were finished. In

> return, Darrow was able to bring to the childless Altgeld some of the good things brought to a father by his son: love, filial respect, an eagerness to learn, an hour spent in the warmth of confidence.2

The book that Altgeld had written in 1884 was very much to the point of the rest of Darrow's life. In it, the author ripped apart the court and penal system with which Darrow was to joust for over forty years. The volume was one of the very first to raise those challenges that seem new even today.3 Altgeld wrote of the penal system:

> It does not deter the young offender, and it seems not to reform nor restrain the old offender.
>
> This being so, one is naturally led to ask whether there is something wrong with the system; whether it is not based on a mistaken principle; whether it is not a great mill which, in one way or another, supplies its own grist, a maelstrom which draws from the outside, and then keeps its victims moving in a circle until swallowed in the vortex.
>
> For it seems, first to make criminals out of many that are not naturally so; and, second, to render it difficult for those once convicted ever to be anything else than criminals; and, third, to fail to repress those that do not want to be anything but criminals.4

Altgeld then proceeded to attack the police, the courts and the penal system for the method of arresting people, the improper and indeterminate sentences, the heavy and discriminatory system of fines, the misuse of the grand jury system and the heavy use of prison labor. He raised technical legal points that Darrow would fight for later in courtrooms and begged for reforms, some of which Darrow would win. More than anything else, however, John Peter Altgeld pointed out to the world, to Chicago and to Clarence Darrow that people charged with crimes are persons, human beings with rights and needs. The tendency of society and of the law was rather to consider them "types" and to run roughshod over their rights and to treat them purely and simply out of fear and vindictiveness.

And while Darrow was to be the great pessimist about the world, he made a vehement exception when it came to the law. He very often said he didn't think the world or people would change, but he did believe the law would.

In 1924, Clarence Darrow would use that optimism in his most eloquent plea, the argument before Judge John R. Caverly to spare the lives of the two teenage "thrill-killers," Richard Loeb and Nathan Leopold:

> Your honor stands between the past and the future. You may hang these boys; you may hang them by the neck until they are dead. But in doing it you will turn your face toward the past. In doing it you are making it harder for every other boy who, in ignorance and darkness, must grope his way through the mazes which only childhood knows...
>
> The easy thing and the popular thing to do is hang my clients. I know it. Men and women who do not think will applaud. The cruel and thoughtless will approve. It will be easy today; but in Chicago, and reaching out over the length and breadth of the land, more fathers and mothers, the human, the kind and the hopeful, who are gaining an understanding and asking questions not only about these poor boys, but about their own—these will join in no acclaim at the death of my clients.5

Reporters say there were tears streaming down the judge's face when Darrow finished his plea. The two boys were not hanged, but rather sentenced to life imprisonment for the murder and to 99 years for the kidnaping.

Clarence Darrow in repeatedly attacking "justice" in this country at its point of ultimate punishment, death, was actually striking at the whole system that Altgeld had first questioned in 1884. With capital punishment as the final step, each one that preceded it was thereby escalated. He went much farther than Altgeld, however, and once told the prisoners in Cook County Jail that none of them should be there and that "all of you do the best you can—and that is evidently not very well." He saw them as no different than himself or others on the outside, only the circumstances were different.6

His greatest talent was his ability to sympathize, to put himself in another man's shoes, even the murderer's. He once said:

> Personally, I never killed anybody that I know of. But I have had a great deal of satisfaction now and then reading obituary notices, and I used to delight, with the rest of my hundred-per-cent patriotic friends, when I saw ten or fifteen thousand Germans being killed in a day.[7]

Like Altgeld, Darrow would repeatedly focus on crime and the criminal. The famed lawyer would take the most desperate of cases from across the country and at least save his clients from the hangman or electric chair.

Also, like his mentor, Clarence Darrow would fight for human rights on many fronts. He was deeply involved, as was Altgeld, in politics. The two men, at different times, would make major blows against the monopolies, particularly the one in control of the street railways in Chicago. Altgeld would fight them first as governor of Illinois, and Darrow as a member of the state legislature and later as a special counsel for the city of Chicago.

Both would join in fighting with Eugene Debs against Pullman in the 1895 strike, Altgeld protecting the constitutional right of the people and Darrow as attorney for Debs and the beleaguered American Railway Union workers.

Ironically, as a member of the legislature, Darrow would vote with tears in his eyes against a pension for Altgeld's widow because he felt it would not be appropriate use of the taxpayers' dollars. His beloved friend would have been proud.

At Altgeld's funeral in 1902, Darrow had eulogized:

> Today we pay our last sad homage to the most devoted lover, the most abject slave, the fondest, wildest, dreamiest victim that ever gave his life to liberty's immortal cause.[8]

If Darrow's language were eloquent, it was partially because of his association with men who loved words and their use, as well as the human spirit. One such was Edgar Lee Masters: poet, historian and

Darrow's law partner. Masters wrote the famous "Spoon River Anthology," including the poem "Ann Rutledge." He subsequently published a history of Chicago.

A far more meaningful relationship, however, was that between Darrow and Eugene Debs. When Debs first met Darrow, the latter was working for the Chicago and North Western Railway and Debs was taking on the most powerful Pullman and the United States government. Debs was bold enough to ask Darrow to quit his job to defend the workers and Darrow was feisty enough to do it.

Of Debs, Clarence Darrow said:

> There may have lived sometime, somewhere, a kindlier, a gentler, more generous man than Eugene V. Debs, but I have never known him. Nor have I read or heard of another.[9]

Darrow defended Debs against the charge of conspiracy as a result of the Pullman strike and subsequently a contempt citation for having refused to obey an injunction. They were winning cleanly when the first case was indefinity postponed (and subsequently dropped). It had been before a jury, but the contempt hearing was before the judge who had issued the injunction. Darrow was surprized to find he didn't have a chance.[10] Eugene Debs got six months.

Debs and Darrow would maintain their friendship and share their idealism and their belief in socialism, a choice that Darrow made not out of certainty that it was right but from the belief that capitalism was wrong. He argued:

> I know that the present system does not work. I know that it makes men greedy and selfish and mean. I know that it stifles every good motive in man. I know that under the present system no one on earth can be as good as he would be. I know that capitalism does not work and never can work.[11]

Whether he was commenting on capitalism or talking to prisoners about why they were in jail, Darrow would stress the power of circumstance and environment on a person's behavior. What, then, made Darrow so sensitive to human needs and rights, to people? What was the environment that grabbed hold of this so-so lawyer in his 30s and turned him into a giant? A major part of the answer has to be Chicago, the Chicago of the 1890s.

Stirred on by Altgeld who so loved Chicago that he would run for mayor of the city against impossible odds and in broken health (and lose), Darrow became enmeshed in the city. He first excited the town when he gave a talk at a Free Trade Convention that Henry George's "single tax" followers held in 1889. He went to work for the city corporation counsel's office in 1890 as special assessment attorney and subsequently as corporation counsel. He had in the meantime thrown himself assiduously into one of Chicago's favorite pastimes, the public lecture or debate. He found himself arguing for the single tax, socialism, poetry, Democratic candidates and freethinking. He might fight a mundane battle for more seats on city streetcars or one for freedom involving the Irish or the Boers in Africa.

The cultural life of Chicago was at its germinating fever, a far cry from his experiences in Ashtabula, and Darrow heated up with it. Of him, at this stage, Irving Stone wrote:

> He became one of the leading young and vigorous cultural lights in Chicago because he was so gentle and genuine and honest, because his love for books and thinking shone through everything he said, because he had the gift of the bold, striking phrase, the delicious chuckle, because he could dramatize literature and knowledge, bring them to life with tenderness and a wallop.[12]

Such credentials are not tickets to most "cultures," at least the ones that pride themselves on their elite and sophisticated base. They were to Chicago's, which was attempting to be "gentle and genuine and honest."

And the more the city's social cause in the 1890s unfolded itself as democracy and the brighter its culture sparked, the more inspired Clarence Darrow became.

The greatest thing that Chicago gave to Darrow was a deep and provocative taste of the good life as being something other than the desire for wealth and fame, which biographers say drove him when he first came to the city. He never lost his desire for either, but repeatedly sublimated them to friendship, culture and democracy, all of which Chicago helped him first experience and exude.

His was the simple language of the Midwest, learned in Ohio, but honed in Chicago. His were the direct politics of the city with which he became so enthralled for 50 years. His were the causes of Chicago and especially its working people. Much of his business came to him through the labor unions of the city. His was the role of David against the Goliaths, a task Chicago itself took on so successfully in these years. Chicago grew and Clarence Darrow matured and they both helped each other. He fit the Chicago mold perhaps better than any other man, but it was partially because he and his friends helped make it.

Darrow didn't get released from this bughouse of a world until March 13, 1938. In his final years he repeatedly attempted to retire but one more provocative case would attract his attention and he would be back in the courtroom. In between such events, he returned to the role of philosopher, lecturer and debater.

In the courtroom, he saved a total of 220 clients from execution in a day when a jury and even more a judge were quick to hang or electrocute someone, especially if he or she were poor and had received bad press.13

His deep convictions and his talent with a jury often compensated for his disorganization and, at times, inattention to some aspects of the law. His ability to grill a witness was never shown better than when he broke down the star witness against William D. "Big Bill" Haywood and Charles Moyer, two labor leader charged with the murder of the former governor of Idaho, Frank Steunenberg.

Darrow's summations to juries were rarely short. This one took 11 hours, but one paragraph from it on shows they weren't boring.

> Gentlemen, let me say this: If this jury believes that Haywood and Moyer met Harry Orchard (the prosecution's main witness) in their room, and without any introduction of any sort, they let Harry Orchard tell them of this murder, and that they then turned and gave him $300—if you believe that story, for God's sake take them out and hang them—they deserve to die. They have not got brains enough to lead any labor movements in the world; they are misfits, and I don't see why they have been alive so long.14

They were acquitted.

During these decades, it was not unusual for labor leaders, radicals and blacks to be put on trial on rather flimsy evidence. It was a tactic because the courts felt an obligation to stand against what they considered a conspiracy. And Darrow defended such people because he saw the courts as the real conspirators and he could often convince a jury of that.

Inevitably, the power of the court was turned on Darrow and he was indicted for allegedly trying to bribe a juror in Los Angeles in 1912. He told the jury that he wasn't guilty, but that, whether he was or not, it wasn't the reason he was being tried. Speaking of the group attempting to get him convicted he argued:

> It is not that any of these men care about bribery, but it is that there never was a chance before, since the world began, to claim that bribery had been committed for the poor. Heretofore, bribery, like everything else, had been monopolized by the rich. But now they thought there was a chance to lay this crime to the poor and "to get" me. Is there any doubt about it?[15]

The jury had no doubt, The two jurors who were thought to be leaning against him were in tears at the end of his speech and the jury took only 32 minutes to acquit Darrow.

Clarence Darrow not only freed clients, he also set precedents, written judicial ones as well as others that were simply changed attitudes in the courtrooms. He successfully, for example, struck at the 1843 legal definition of insanity as being based simply on a person's ability to distinguish right from wrong. It would not be until 1954 that the courts would come up with a better definition in recognizing that an "unlawful act" could be the "product of mental disease or mental defect." This simple insight that made use of psychology was one that Darrow had persuaded juries to accept.

Likewise, he fought against the court's definition of its right to arbitrarily use injunctions in strikes and contempt citations to enforce them. Again, it would not be until many years after his death that the Supreme Court would at least partially recognize his position.

In his tangle with William Jennings Bryan in the famous Scopes "Monkey Trial," the issue was the right of his client to teach evolution.

Technically, he lost as his client was found guilty of violating Tennessee law and was fined. Darrow and the teacher, however, won favorable publicity for the concepts of evolution and the rights of teachers far beyond their highest hopes.

As early as 1912, Darrow staunchly protested against wiretapping and bugging, just as soon as the tools were invented to do it with. He argued:

> Wouldn't it be better that every rogue and rascal in the world should go unpunished than to say that detectives could put a dictograph into your parlor, in your dining room, in your bedroom and destroy that privacy which alone makes life worth living?[16]

But, more than any other, Clarence Darrow's challenge was that someday the courts ,the legislature, or even the people might courageously strike down capital punishment. He summed up the issue behind it in a 1924 debate:

> In the end, this question is simply one of the humane feelings against the brutal feelings. One who likes to see suffering, out of what he thinks is a righteous indignation, or any other, will hold fast to capital punishment. One who has sympathy, imagination, kindness and understanding, will hate it and detest it as he hates and detests death.[17]

The fact that one good lawyer—Clarence Darrow—could save 220 men and women from capital punishment proved decisively that the system was neither equal nor fair enough to be used to take a man's life.

Perhaps the even greater accomplishment was that Darrow—cynic that he was—never became embittered, and that—complicated as he was—his faith in the people remained so simple.

To those who scoff at democracy, the greatest contradiction has to be one person who becomes a democrat and who stays that way.

Clarence Darrow is Chicago's lasting argument for a democratic lifestyle and culture.

1. Darrow was so very quotable that reading almost any material about him and especially by him is rewarding. This particular quote is from the International News Service obituary written for newspaper reference files before his death. Other biographical information in this chapter comes from other contemporary newspaper clips, from his semi-autobiographical work "Farmington" (A. C. McClurg & Co., 1904), "Clarence Darrow for the Defense" by Irving Stone (Doubleday, Doran & Co., 1941) and especially "Attorney for the Damned: Clarence Darrow in His Own Word" edited by Arthur Weinberg (Simon and Shuster, 1957). His actual autobiography (often inaccurate) is "The Story of My Life" (Charles Scribner's Sons, 1934), written on a trip to Europe when he had no recourse to checks and sources.

2. Actually works out numbers.

3. "Our Penal Machinery and Its Victims" (1884) was reprinted in Altgeld's "Live Questions" Vol. I (Donohue & Hennelberry, 1890). Initially, it was reviewed—according to Harry Barnard in "Eagle Forgotten" (Bobbs-Merrill, 1938)—by only one newspaper, the *Chicago Times*. The reviewer criticized it for not taking into account "that certain strains of blood constantly contribute to the criminal classes." Its sensitivity and influence may be said to put this pamphlet in a place in the Chicago Democratic evolution comparable to Thomas Paine's "Common Sense" in the American Revolution.

4. "Live Questions" p.162.

5. Arthur Weinberg, ed. "Attorney for the Damned" p.86.

6. Arthur Weinberg in his Darrow compilation reprinted this famous lecture. He tells us that Darrow's friends were distressed with him espousing such theories to the inmates of the jail. Undaunted, he had the speech printed in pamphlet form that sold for 5 cents. He then wrote in typical inverted Darrow-style an introduction that stated the "good paper and somewhat expensive form" of the pamphlet would place it "only before those whose intelligences and affluence will prevent them from being influenced by it." You can't help but believe some people took that introduction seriously. The Charles H. Kerr Company of Chicago currently has it in print.

7. This quote is from an Associated Press standing obituary on Darrow. Incredibly, Clarence Darrow got temporarily euchred out of his pacifist position at the time of America's entry into World War I, according to Irving Stone "Clarence Darrow for the Defense" (Doubleday, Doran and Company, 1941) p.356-9. Pictures which were shown to him supposedly of German atrocities had much to do with his change. The government of Great Britain subsequently selected him as the American it most wanted to propagandize further. That nation invited and hosted him for a five-month, mid-war visit. The British failed. He went there "hating German warriors" and returned sympathetic "to the German young boys forced to go to war." He subsequently fought for the

rights of conscientious objectors, arousing both anger and hatred. Altgeld, "The Cost of Something for Nothing" (Chicago Historical Bookworks, 1989) Appendix p.1.

8. Stone, p.52.

9. Stone (p.64) said Darrow "Had failed to go back to the beginnings of the Supreme Court, to trace its consistent efforts to defend and entrench property rights in the development of American life."

10. The quote is from his summation to the jury in the 1920 trial of Communists in Chicago ("Attorney for the Damned," p.139). By comparison, his comments in a 1911 debate show his ability to look at the same thing from multiple vantage points: "You cannot demonstrate any theory of society the way you demonstrate the multiplication table, unless it is Socialism—and you cannot demonstrate that in the same way unless you are speaking to an audience of Socialists. You might demonstrate Single Tax to a Single Taxer, but you could not do it to anyone else." The debate was published by the Charles H. Kerr Co. and titled "Marx Versus Tolstoy: A Debate." The publishing firm is a Chicago-based "co-operative" that published many democratic or Socialist pieces that would not have been touched by any other company.

11. Ibid. p.31.

12. Darrow did have one client who was hanged, but he defended him only on his appeal, not at his original trial. The case was in the late 1890s.

13. Weinberg, p.482.

14. Weinberg, p.496.

15. Weinberg, p.516. His irritation in the matter was personal, as a dictophone was used in an attempt to trap him in connection with the McNamara Case. The quote is from his defense when he was indicted and tried for allegedly attempting to bribe a juror in the case.

16. "Debate on Capital Punishment," (Little Blue Books No.883, 1924) p.63.

Epilogue: An End and a Beginning

In 1917, Chicago took its major product, democracy, off the market. Since 1895, it was free with the air of Chicago or had sold along with newspapers for a penny. War seemed to inflate the price beyond the reach of the American people.

The Night Chicago Died

In 1974, a recording by a British group became number one in Chicago as well as in other cities across the United States. The refrain was: "The night Chicago died...I heard my Mama cry...the night Chicago died!"

"The Night Chicago Died" by the group Paper Lace was a "platinum single," which means that it sold 2 million plus records. The setting was supposed to be the city's gangster era and the events to take place on "Chicago's East Side." Technically, the city's East Side is Lake Michigan, but an area far southeast in Chicago refers to itself as the "East Side." That is the only half-way authentic fact about "The Night Chicago Died."

People, as the promoters and advertisers like to say, "identified." Never mind that the other words of the song were inconsequential and inaccurate, it was an opportunity to emote about Chicago's tragedy. For, indeed, somehow, somewhere around 1917, a part of Chicago had died. Many people seem to have a pent-up vague awareness of that death.

In his book, "Chicago: City on the Make," Nelson Algren inferred that it was Chicago's soul that had died.

What the city lost is more easily recoverable than its soul, however. It is the spirit of going to the people as the source of art, literature, language, architecture, merchandizing, government, culture, law and the solution to social problems.

Chicago lost its strength when it surrendered its faith in its poorest citizen.

The critics of Chicago in reviewing its literary and cultural demise overlook that simple fact.

Nelson Algren came close to saying it, but then he got so mad at the newspapers.[1]

Nevertheless, Algren has to be taken very seriously in his analysis of Chicago because he wrote that he loves Chicago (he later moved to New Jersey) and not many great writers passionately admit that they love Chicago in this era.

He wrote:

> Before you earn the right to rap any sort of joint, you have to love it a little while. You have to belong to Chicago like a crosstown transfer out of the Armitage Avenue barns first; and you can't rap it then just because you've been crosstown.[2]
>
> Yet if you've tried New York for size and put in a stint in Paris, lived long enough in New Orleans to get the feel of the docks and belonged to the old Marseille awhile, if the streets of Naples have warmed you and those of London have chilled you, if you've seen the terrible green African light moving low over the Sudan or even passed hurriedly through Cincinnati—then Chicago is your boy at last and you can say it and make it stick:
>
> That it's a backstreet, backslum loudmouth whose challenges go ringing around the world like any green punk around any neighborhood bar...[3]

Algren also saw Chicago as "the sleepless city Dreiser and Sherwood Anderson found; that [novelist James] Farrell was born in; that Richard Wright came to because he had no other place to go."

He further described it as "The Middle City,[4] the place where the individual American conscience and formalized opinion had found its sharpest division. The American spirit has discovered its manliest voices as well as its meanest here."

In these descriptions, he was speaking of the past. In the present (he was writing in the early 1950's), his adjectives more often were "punk" and "mediocre."

Algren scored bitterly the city that had abandoned Walt Whitman's offer, bred by hard times on the Middle Border, that "If you tire, give me both burdens" and the Chicago that had forgotten Eugene Debs saying, "While there is a soul in prison I am not free." He was hurt that the town

"While there is a soul in prison I am not free." He was hurt that the town was no longer an audience for his own works, which were written in the spirit of, "I belong to those convicts and prostitutes myself."

Algren accused the high and the mighty of killing the spirit of Chicago, and in particular, the newspapers.[5] But that very spirit had only strengthened itself in Debs, Altgeld, Addams, Darrow, Sullivan, and Sandburg, when they had faced an even more hostile Chicago press. They grew from from the very opposition that he claimed killed their heritage.

Algren for all the ferocity of his words said he loved Chicago or "the joint," as he called it. He therefore could not have truly believed the city's democratic spirit deserved to have its death certificate signed, sealed and delivered.

Christopher Morley, who visited the city in the mid-1930s, still found soul and spirit in Chicago, which he described thus:

> She is unruly at heart; more than a little goofy; she will be one of the last to be tamed by the slow frost of correctness. The persecution of cruel climate and economic zigzag are likely to keep her temperament at extremes...She spikes the small beer of living with the pure alcohol of the impossible.[6]

Morley added in his book, "Old Loopy: A Love Letter for Chicago:"

> I think she had less hypocrisy, less prudential qualms than some of her Eastern neighbors. She admits more the impulses of love, laughter, lunacy—even of anger, greed and fear—which make up life.[7]

The newspapers were critical of Algren for being critical of Chicago and both parties were wrong. Chicago is not suffering from too much criticism, but rather from a lack of the kind of love that Christopher Morley was directing himself toward.

Chicago still has many of its tools. It still has the language that is most universally American. If an further advance is to be made in behalf of the American vernacular, the tradition and the opportunity is in Chicago.

It has been said of its writers at the turn-of-the-century that they came to Chicago riding the rails and left in Pullman coaches. Algren in the 1960s wrote that they bought one-way tickets out of O'Hare International Airport. A city can afford to lose good writers and artists as long as it attracts new young talents and "traps" a handful of great ones. That entrapment can come in the form of love for the city or some crazy, unique limitations in the artist that Chicago can compensate for. Altgeld, Darrow, Addams, Field, Sandburg, Sullivan, Harriet Monroe and opera diva Mary Garden all became trapped by the city or by their love for it.[8]

Chicago found itself as a city in the Chicago Fire of 1871 and then even more so in the martyrdom of the defendants in the Haymarket trial of 1887. The blood of the men convicted and hanged—not for shooting of policemen in the event but for "conspiracy" by preaching dissidence with the established order in Chicago—became the standard by which Chicago democrats in the next generation could measure themselves. Men and women like Altgeld, Addams and Sullivan were not found wanting.

The true democrats were true to their art (or politics), and believed in the people.[9] Thcy were not being mesmerized by money, prestige or "clout."

Altgeld and others warned, "freebies" have to be recognized as a deliberate effort by people with a luke-warm taste for democracy tocontrol art and culture. What is incredible is how often they are successful.[10]

The teacher, the artist and the politician find blandishments disabling. Clarence Darrow learned this truth from Altgeld. John Dewey experienced it through his friends Francis Parker and Jane Addams. Frank Lloyd Wright's style had as its teacher "Der Meister," Louis Sullivan. The ultimate free ride is offered by thepropaganda of war, as Clarence Darrow and others found out in World War I.

In his book, "The Second City," A. J. Liebling reinforces the contention that World War I helped stifle Chicago's message. He quoted a woman phone caller who told him that Chicago's decline should be dated from "the day Jane Addams boarded the Henry Ford Peace Ship in 1916.

"The intellectual life, as well as the social conscience of Chicago," she continued, "centered on Jane Addams and Hull House in the years before World War I. Miss Addams' pacifism destroyed much of her prestige and consequently that of her whole group. Momentum carried some of the writers through the early twenties, and then they dispersed, having nothing to hold them together."[11]

The Jane Addams incident was relevant, but the meaning was sorely misunderstood by the caller. First of all, Jane Addams never went on the ship.[12] World War I in Europe was a war chosen by, and fought in behalf of, aristocratic powers. America—as a burgeoning democracy—had no relevance in providing war matériel or taking sides in the conflict.

The mayor of Chicago, Big Bill Thompson—from the standpoint of political corruption, probably the city's worst—had no trouble seeing that the United States had no place in the war, but the Eastern-bred President of the United States—for all his theoretical talk of Democracy—let this nation become involved in the war. And to do so, democracy had to become sloganized and the control of the country taken from the hands of the people and put into those of the war machine.

America is still challenged to become disenchanted with the chauvinism and slogans it created in World War I and called "patriotism." It is faced with an opportunity to consider the strength of its purpose rather than the power of its money or military might.

The ultimate challenge for America is to respect and empower its people, as Chicago once showed it could.

1. The quotes from Nelson Algren's "Chicago: City on the Make" are all from what is known as the "Contact Edition." It was published in 1961, 10 years after the book was first issued and contained a new prefatory article from which several quotes in this chapter are taken.

2. The style here is best described as "pure Algren." His biographers, Martha Cox and Wayne Chatterton, in their book "Nelson Algren" (Twayne, 1975), say of this book and these quotes: "Algren fuses 'metaphorical fireworks' and poetic syntax into prose paragraphs whose substance in often the mundane, harsh, or even cynical sociohistoryiography of his material. The effect is unlike that of any other work in American letters." And that does not seem to be an overstatement.

3. Algren not only "bummed" his way through these places during the Depression but experienced many of the incidents that would appear in his book "Walk on the Wild Side," including working a con game by selling phony certificates for "free" beauty parlor treatment.

4. "City on the Make, " p.52.

5. The term "Middle City" for Chicago and "Middle Border" for the Midwest were popular for many years but few if any noted writers subsequent to Algren who used them.

6. Specifically, Algren's enemies were the *Chicago Daily News* and the *Chicago Tribune*, but he didn't like the others either. The *Tribune* now sponsors a short story contest in his name.

7. "Old Loopy" (The Argus Book Shop, 1935) p.16.

8. Ibid. p.13. Christopher Morley's book is very short and is far from incisive about Chicago as was that of his fellow Englishman's William T. Stead, who had visited a different world fair in Chicago 40 years earlier and then wrote "If Christ Came to Chicago."

9. John Peter Altgeld, Clarence Darrow and Jane Addams were all involved in the release and pardon of those convicted but not hanged in the Haymarket trial. The impact on the others of the trial and aftermath on others is illustrated in Sandburg's life. As Harry Golden points out in his biography of his friend, "Carl Sandburg became a radical in 1893, the day Governor John P. Altgeld extended a pardon to the surviving Haymarket rioters." Golden's language was unfortunate, it should be noted, in calling the imprisoned men "rioters."

10. John Peter Altgeld, "The Cost of Something fcr Nothing" (Chicago Historical Bookworks reprint, 1989).

11. "The Second City' (Alfred A. Knopf, 1952) p.13.

12. The story of the Peace Ship itself is more sad than quixotic. Henry Ford proved no strong leader of men and the many groups and strong personalities aboard the ship clashed and the whole venture became the object

of international ridicule. In some ways, it may have hastened America's move away from neutrality because it put pacifism in such a bad light and tainted other war resisters' hopes for a negotiated peace.

Index